TALES FROM THE COUCH

TALES FROM THE COUCH

A CLINICAL PSYCHOLOGIST'S TRUE STORIES OF PSYCHOPATHOLOGY

BOB WENDORF, PsyD

Carrel Books may be purchased in bulk at special discounts for sales promotion, corporate gifts, fund-raising, or educational purposes. Special editions can also be created to specifications. For details, contact the Special Sales Department, Carrel Books, 307 West 36th Street, 11th Floor, New York, NY 10018 or carrelbooks@skyhorsepublishing.com.

Carrel Books® is a registered trademark of Skyhorse Publishing, Inc.®, a Delaware corporation.

Visit our website at www.carrelbooks.com.

10 9 8 7 6 5 4 3 2 1

Library of Congress Cataloging-in-Publication Data is available on file.

Cover Design: Owen Corrigan

ISBN: 978-1-63144-025-0

Ebook ISBN: 978-1-63144-030-4

Printed in the United States of America

This book is dedicated to my patients, without whom it could not
have been written,
And to my friend and former student Jay Pesek, without whom it
would not have been published.

CONTENTS

INTRODUCTION

ACTUALLY, PEOPLE ARE OFTEN DISAPPOINTED to find that my office contains no couch. The couch is a psychoanalytic furnishing with a classically Freudian slip-cover. I'm not all that Freudian myself. I see a lot of kids, and a couch invites either bouncing or lounging or sibling conflict, none of which is useful to my work. I see a lot of married couples, and a couch puts them too close together to deal with their areas of conflict. You don't fight with somebody you're sharing a seat with. So there's no couch. If I did have a couch I'd be tempted to nap on it, as one of my partners occasionally does, and that's not my way of practicing psychology either. Sorry, but the couch in this book's title is strictly metaphorical.

What I do have is thirty-six years of experience in clinical psychology. I've seen patients in hospitals, residential treatment centers, university counseling centers, community mental health centers, my private office, schools, their homes, even my own home. I've developed specialties in marriage and family therapy, child and adolescent therapy, ADHD, eating disorders, pain management, and multiple personality disorder. Seems as if every time I develop a sub-specialty, the insurance companies decide they no longer want to pay for it. The result, however, is that I've had a very broad range of experience and met all kinds of patients. I've seen a guy who had sex with dead animals on the road-side and a woman whose neurofibromatosis left huge masses growing off her body almost like clusters of brown grapes. I faced a man with a rifle, who'd been laid off for fighting at work and was threatening to kill somebody. I worked with a couple where the wife was positive her husband was faithful, but he told me privately he crept off to see his paramour while she slept. No serial killers, thank God, but I've seen most everything else.

I've had opportunities to witness unusual events and meet fascinating people I'd never have experienced outside of psychology. I was brought into the operating room to view a coronary by-pass so I could knowledgeably interview patients for a training film. The man's heart was an arm's length away, as I chit-chatted with his surgeons like somebody from a *M.A.S.H.* episode. Another time I held the hand of a schizophrenic patient as a carcinoma was carved off her nose. I got liberally sprayed with blood on that occasion, and the smell of her arteries being cauterized made me a bit green in the face, but she wouldn't allow the procedure without my presence.

The inspiration for this book came from my son Marc and his wild and crazy friends Wes, Chris, and Creighton, who loved to hear stories of the strange and fascinating patients I've seen. The book is a compilation of some of my most interesting and entertaining cases, and, I hope, a quick summary of what they have taught me about life and the human condition. Some are funny and some bizarre; some are gross and some tragic. But all these stories are about real people, even if I've altered the tales a bit and changed patients' names to protect their confidentiality. The people in this book are real, and their struggles and agonies and sorrows and triumphs are all real. I want them to know that I respect their efforts, share in their accomplishments, regret their failures—and mine—and value them as fellow rafters on the white-waters of life. They've been my career and my life, and I appreciate them all, even the ones who've called me at midnight to say they're NOT suicidal, or have thrown up in my trash can, or just came in to flirt with my office manager. The work gets tedious at times, and the paperwork onerous;

managed care is diligently trying to destroy my profession; it's not a royal road to riches; and you meet some truly obnoxious, even dangerous people. But psychologists rarely complain of boredom.

I've been listening to people tell me their stories for thirty-six years. Thank you for listening now to my own tales—"from the couch."

A Word about Confidentiality and Terminology

AS I'VE SAID, THESE STORIES are all about real people, people who have been my patients. Thus, I have an ethical and legal, as well as a moral, duty to protect their privacy and respect their confidence. I have tried to do that in every way I can, by changing their names, altering their professions, and revising the facts of their cases in various other ways. It's been difficult for some of the stories, as the true facts are essential for understanding the clinical dynamics of the cases. My Asperger's patient, for example could not have been transformed into a Sinatra impersonator; it's Elvis or it makes no sense. Thus, it is conceivable that a reader might be able to identify one of these patients, and thereby gain access to privileged information, despite my best efforts to prevent this. Should that happen, I would beg such a reader to keep the information to himself, and I apologize if I have done anyone any harm. My purpose in telling these stories is purely to inform and entertain my readers. I've been psychologically accurate, and all the events and characters I've described are real. But in my telling of these stories, doctors become lawyers, geography has been shifted, and patient characteristics have occasionally been re-assigned. For example, I did indeed put two MPD patients in the same hospital room—but not necessarily the two I've described.

So, even if you think you know someone, the new facts you discover may well belong to someone else.

Some readers may object to certain terms that appear in this book. It is certainly not my intention to offend. I maintain that psychiatry (and other fields) have played the "name game" for too long, pretending to make progress while simply retitling the same conditions. For example, "mental retardation" (which, in its literal sense, is a fairly accurate term) replaced formerly technical terms that had come to have a pejorative connotation. "Idiot" and "moron" were both proper medical terms with precise definitions. Now "mentally retarded" has similarly been rejected as unacceptable in favor of "mentally challenged." Likewise, changing from "Manic-Depressive Disorder" to "Bipolar Disorder" reflects no progress in understanding the condition itself. In fact, I find the new term misleading.

Of course, one day soon the new terminology may be rejected. In all of these cases, the condition is unchanged, no matter the name. I have used terminology that was common when I practiced, and that is commonly used by many practitioners today.

M.A.S.H. got it right. This is the way both doctors and patients talk.

CHAPTER ONE
Ping-Pong Therapy

"WILLIAM" WAS MY FIRST "REAL" patient. Not just somebody to test or a phony interview with a classmate, but a real human patient of my very own. I was doing my internship a bit out of sequence, preferring the Illinois prairie to the swamps, rice paddies, and verdant hills of Vietnam. The facility was a state-run residential treatment center for adolescents, and William had already been there for twice our average length of stay. His assignment to me wasn't a vote of confidence in my clinical acumen; everybody else had already had a shot at him, and I was next in line.

William was a gaunt, slight sixteen-year-old, with a bomb-shaped nose smashed into an artillery range of a face. He was well-behaved, indeed helpful and cooperative, but he kept to himself and rarely spoke (partly to hide his poor dentition). He was barely literate, had no known talents, and had dropped out of school. William's father had abandoned the family, and his mother supported them by prostituting herself in the family living room, often with the kids in attendance. William had no other family to turn to, so he moved into the large dog house out back, sharing it with his only friend, a loyal German Shepherd. William was hospitalized for depression after the dog got run over by a truck. I knew him for nearly a year before I ever saw William smile. My graduate program at Champaign-Urbana was very behaviorally oriented, and the hospital I was working in was run by several faculty members. The Program for Adolescent and Community Education (PACE) was a model behavior modification program. But William was a special case. His behavior was fine and needed no modification. His thoughts and feelings were the areas in need of change, and frankly, there wasn't a lot to work with. I really didn't know where to start, and my limited training wasn't much help. I talked with William about the problem, figuring he might have some goals or plans of his own. I knew he needed something to feel good about, but nothing presented itself.

So, I asked him, "William, what do you have to be happy about?"

"Nothing," he said. "My father dumped us. My mother is turning tricks in front of us. My dog is dead. I didn't graduate from school and I've got no job and no money. Nobody likes me."

"What do you like about yourself?" I plunged ahead, thinking, "We've got to get you some self-esteem somewhere."

"Nothing," he answered. "I'm ugly; I'm stupid; I got no friends. There is nothing about me or my life that I like."

"Okay," I persisted, "then what are you good at?"

"Nothing," he said. "I can't read very good; I can't do anything at sports or shoot pool or do anything. I can't even drive a car."

Even a rookie psychologist knows you can't talk somebody out of feeling depressed. You can't convince him he's a great guy and should feel happy, especially somebody holding the cards William had drawn. There wasn't much point in arguing with him; it would only hurt my credibility. The truth was that William was essentially correct. He wasn't very bright (low IQ); he was a dropout; he had no family worth claiming. He had no job skills, no friends, and no sex appeal. He couldn't catch a fly with a honey-covered mitt. So I agreed with him.

"Alright, we haven't got much to go on," I conceded. "But we have got to find you some way to be happy and something to be happy with yourself about. So you're not good at anything now, but maybe we can teach you something. So what would you *like* to be good at?"

"Ping-pong," said William, after a moment's thought. "I'd like to be good at ping-pong. I wanna be the best player on the Boys' Unit."

Now, this selection was not so bizarre as it might seem on first hearing. This was the windswept Illinois prairie town of Decatur, "Soybean Capital of the World," where the temperature routinely drops to twenty below and there isn't a hill between you and the North Pole to take even an edge off the sinus-stabbing gale. The Boys' Unit housed fifteen to twenty testosterone-inflamed, girl-deprived, and legally challenged adolescents. These guys needed to work out, blow off steam, and compete with each other on a regular basis. We had a small gym and a billiards room, but we had to share them with several other units. The swimming pool was down for repairs, and video games were twenty years in the future. We played football in the snow until it got over a foot deep. Then all that was left to us, reliably, predictably, daily, was ping-pong. It was the "National Pastime" of the Boys' Unit. Reputations were won and lost at the ping-pong table. Fights broke out over bad calls or illegal serves. We even played "Nerf" ping-pong late at night with a large spongey ball. (It actually worked surprisingly well, but the utter silence made for an eerie game.) I used to chop delinquent punks down to size by beating them at ping-pong, left-handed and sitting in a desk chair.

But that was much later. At the time of this discussion I was at best a mediocre player. William, I'm afraid, was pathetic. Fortunately, I was naive and cocky, so I took up the gauntlet (or the paddle) and promised to transform him into the deadliest player on the Unit. William looked at me like *I* needed to be hospitalized, but also with the first tentative spark of enthusiasm and hope I'd seen yet.

"When do we start?" he asked.

"Now," I said, and we adjourned to the table tennis arena.

William and I played ping-pong at every opportunity. Our "individual therapy" sessions were conducted at the ping-pong table. I even connived to hold a few "group therapy" sessions as doubles matches. We took a "therapeutic leave of absence" (field trip) to the local sporting goods store, where we spent our respective allowances on a couple of smooth-rubber-sided all-pro paddles. No semi-shredded sandpaper paddles for us. We made a trek to the library and found a book that showed us how to use our new weapons. We practiced top-spin smashes and back-spin defenses and learned how to put a truly nasty hook on our serves. As it happened, the Chinese National Team was touring the Midwest, and William and I went to see and study them. They were awe-inspiring. William and I were doing ping-pong therapy, and we were going after it hell-bent-for-leather (or rubber) with six-guns (paddles) blazing. We were working at this as if it were a life or death struggle, because for William it was.

Of course, there was a lot of conversation, too—over the table, in study sessions, and in post-game wrap-ups. We got to know each other pretty well, William and I. William learned to trust me. I learned to like and respect him. We talked over and reprocessed his life history and his sense of himself. He learned to think of himself differently and to see that his wretched lot was not his fault. William finally had a friend and a mentor and a father surrogate. William was not a gifted natural athlete, but he was a tough little guy, and he worked like a young associate trying to make partner. In a few months William had former street-fighters begging for mercy on the green-netted battlefield. As a doubles team he and I were destroying seasoned competitors, putting my internship in some peril as we took on the Director and Internship Coordinator. William had arrived. He was a power to be respected in an arena where it mattered. People wanted to know him. Yet, he still never smiled.

Then, slowly, I witnessed one of the most remarkable transformations I've ever seen. Over a period of just a couple of weeks, the dour, glowering sour-puss William metamorphosed into one of the happiest kids I've ever known. As he learned to accept my affection and approval, William learned to like himself. As he developed an area of not just skill, but mastery, he learned to respect and value himself. And that opened him up to the affection and approval of others, which had always been available, but invisible to him. He became a kind of Unit mascot, well-liked and well-regarded by staff and students alike. William was happy and rarely stopped grinning. And he didn't look so homely when he grinned.

There was still a lot of work to be done. William was a dropout, with no job skills, no family, and no money. He was learning to like himself, to trust, to be happy. But he was still pretty fragile. He needed some good training and he needed a mother's touch. Fortunately, that's when Sallie stepped in to help.

My favorite co-therapist at that time was Sallie Brewer, a sweet, gutsy young woman, whose husband Fred was off in Korea. Sallie had a lot of cats, but no kids, and she was a born Momma. She took William in and loved him like a pound puppy. She brought him home to care for her cats and mow her lawn. Between us, we helped him get his GED, then earn an associate's degree in plumbing. Before long, William was a master plumber making twice the salary I got. And he had a family. When Fred came home from Korea, he turned out to be grouchy in the early morning, but otherwise a great dad. William had a good and loving family for the first time in his life. And he was happy. I treated my first patient with ping-pong therapy, and it worked.

I learned a lot from William (and from Fred and Sallie). I learned that behavior therapy is not the only, or necessarily the best, approach to treatment, though it's just the thing for some cases. I learned that self-esteem is essential to good mental health and that it comes from yourself and that it's *very* subjective. You learn to value yourself based on criteria you choose yourself. I learned that good people can come from very bad families, especially if they have a little help. I realized that sometimes you have to go outside the usual boundaries of the traditional therapeutic relationship and that real human relationships are the real therapy. I learned that I can't do it all by myself, that I need professional support, and that ultimately the patient must come to his own sense of self-worth. And I learned that magical transformations can happen with good therapy. People can change. I also learned to play a fairly respectable game of ping-pong, with either hand. (You can always spot a veteran of adolescent residential treatment: they can play at least competent pool and good ping-pong.) It was a good first case, even if it left me with a pretty odd sense of what therapy is all about.

CHAPTER TWO
Bad Boys and Girls

MY INTERNSHIP IN ADOLESCENT TREATMENT was largely a matter of staying in school, avoiding the war in Vietnam, and getting some fortuitously good training. I never actually decided to specialize in this area of psychology. In fact, I never took a course in child or adolescent psychology. There's a cautionary tale here: my internship led to a first job with a child guidance clinic in Austin, Texas, then to Coordinator of Child and Adolescent Services at a Birmingham community mental health center, and eventually to Director of an inpatient adolescent unit—though I never chose or trained for Child Psychology. So be careful in selecting your first job. I did find that I liked treating children and adolescents. In fact, I actually like adolescents, especially somebody else's adolescents. Your own are more difficult to deal with. I even like and relate to "bad" teenagers, probably because I see in them my own rebellious side.

My internship at PACE gave me plenty of exposure to "bad" adolescents, and I found that I liked and sympathized with many of them. Of course, I was barely out of my own adolescence, if at all. There's a continuing debate in psychiatry and in our society at large as to what constitutes the difference between a criminal and an insane person. To what extent should people be held accountable for their misconduct? What if there are mitigating circumstances? Where there is clear physical pathology which causes misbehavior, no one would hold the miscreant liable. That wouldn't be fair, because it isn't his fault. For example, I saw a young woman in Austin who would go into sudden rages and punch walls, break down doors, smash china, and hit people. Finding that she also suffered from severe headaches and that she couldn't even remember her outbursts, I sent her to a neurologist. He confirmed my hunch that she had a seizure disorder which caused her to act out violently. Truly, it was not under her control and not her fault. It was caused by a brain storm. Fortunately, an anticonvulsant medication stopped her rage episodes entirely. Then we did some psychotherapy to address her shaken sense of self. Similarly, a tiny minority of schizophrenic patients hear voices telling them to kill people and slice them up for luncheon meat. They are found "not guilty by reason of insanity" and remanded to the custody of the Department of Mental Health, not the Department of Corrections. Rightly so, as schizophrenia is a disease of the brain, not a moral failure.

On the other hand, what if you intentionally produce the neurological condition which leads to behavior truly out of your control? A drunk driver can be guilty of vehicular homicide even though he had no idea what he was doing behind the wheel. Again, rightly so. You choose to drink and drive, you live with the consequences, even given the persuasive argument that alcoholism is itself a partially inherited disease. So is lung cancer, but you probably won't get it if you don't *choose* to smoke. Then there's my patient Dwayne, who suffers from a legitimate manic-depressive psychosis, but also has a great fondness for cocaine. Dwayne does a little "blow" and gets a touch of cocaine grandiosity. He quits taking his lithium and goes into a full-blown manic psychosis in which he thinks he's God's personal bodyguard. He gets rowdy, gets busted, and ends up in jail, then tries to get me to commit him to the state hospital. Dwayne is a one-man philosophy course on causality and ethics. (He is described further in Chapter Eight on "Truly Crazy People.")

Every prison is full of people with Attention Deficit Hyperactivity Disorder, which we believe to be an inherited disorder of impulse control. How accountable are they for their crimes? Does the under-functioning of their frontal lobes excuse their misconduct? And there is the "social disease" argument for the influence of poverty and early family experiences on delinquent behavior (made famous by Officer Krupke in *West Side Story*).

It is well documented that impoverished and violent neighbor-hoods, not to mention criminal families, turn out children with high rates of delinquency. Even divorce puts children at higher risk. Are these kids at fault? And if not, how does one account for the fact that some very good people come from the same ghettos and alleyways as the gangsters? Does the distinction between evil and insanity even make consistent sense? It is interesting to note that communication theorist Paul Watzlawick finds that human beings naturally tend to ascribe bad faith to someone with whom they are miscommunicating. That is, they assume the other is either malevolent ("bad") or crazy ("mad") when all that has occurred is a simple misunderstanding of what is being said. How many of our patients or prisoners are simply misunderstood? At PACE we thought a lot about such issues, as we got to know these delinquent and/or crazy adolescents as real people. We thought even more about how we could help them get better.

"O.J." (not the football player/alleged murderer) was a good exam-ple of the task we faced, an adolescent who'd been labeled both bad and mad. We found him on a back ward for the violently retarded, so doped up on Mellaril he could barely speak. O.J. was big and black and tough, and he'd grown up on the wrong side of Champaign's University Boulevard. So when he pretty naturally drifted into some minor delin-quencies, he'd been diagnosed mentally retarded and locked away. He was on enough daily neuroleptic medication to keep you and me both unconscious for a week. We brought him to PACE and discontinued all his antipsychotic meds. He was nearly eighteen and very street-wise. Frankly, I thought it was a bad idea to admit him.

I was vindicated in my judgment almost immediately, though only temporarily. As soon as he regained normal consciousness O.J. took over the Unit. Staff and student alike were completely intimidated, and for good reason. O.J. got crossways with another intern, for example, picked the man up, and flipped him over, sweeping the floor with his long hippie curls. When he got aggressive or out of control, we threw him in the "jug," a bare-walled, tile-floored lock-up with a two-by-four barring the door. But it took at least six of us to do it, as O.J. was fond of remarking, while strutting triumphantly into time-out. He quickly established an efficient protection racket to extort favors from the other patients: pay up or beat up were the only options. Far from being retarded, O.J. was slick, too. He was rarely seen actually hitting anybody, and he kept his insolence and disdain a bare half-step short of the punishable limit. We had Danny, a former college lineman, on our staff, but otherwise O.J. was "The Man."

Then two incidents changed the whole picture, and O.J., dramatically. I was unlucky enough to catch O.J. swatting another patient, a "jug-able" offense. And I was even unluckier to be alone, sitting in the "store" where patients traded in their good behavior tokens for meal tickets, passes to the pool hall, TV privileges, and so on.

"I saw that, O.J.," I was compelled to say. "Hit the jug."

O.J. glowered at me and didn't move. "I ain't going nowhere," he said.

"Fine," I replied. "Since you won't go voluntarily, you owe me forty minutes instead of twenty. Get moving." I managed to say it fairly convincingly, but I was getting pretty nervous. There was no backup in sight.

O.J. sauntered on into the store, his six-foot, two-inch body looming menacingly over me. "I'm not going nowhere," he vowed, "and if you try to make me, I'm gonna beat the shit out of you."

He could have done it. I was in good shape, but of average build and utterly unskilled in the pugilistic arts. And I was scared. I could only hope these facts would escape his notice. So I glared back at him in my most authoritarian manner and said, "No, you're not. You're going to do as I say, and if you lay a finger on me, I'm going to put you right through that window. Now I said *move*." It was the first time I'd learned to use "The Voice," the voice of command which would serve me well in my stint as Adolescent Unit Director twelve years later. It was a good bluff, but that's about all.

Fortunately, O.J. was suddenly confused and uncertain. In his whole life nobody had ever spoken to him in this manner. Adults had either ignored and neglected him, confronted him as a threat, or screamed abusively at him. No one had ever acted towards him like an authority figure. Like a parent. He didn't know what to do. So he mumbled, "aw, shit," turned and shuffled slowly into the jug. I slammed home the locking bar and tried to keep my knees from shaking too visibly.

Incident number two was his confrontation with Sallie, the therapist who'd helped me with "William." Same basic scenario, same basic results, only Sallie—all 98 pounds of her—told him she'd scratch his eyes out. As with me, he retreated to the safety of the jug. He had over a foot on her in height and more than doubled her weight, but O.J. knew when he was out-gunned.

After that, O.J.'s behavior began to improve. There were some more fisticuffs and some further defiance, but never with Sallie nor me. And when he was confronted, O.J. took it with good graces, even a wry "okay, you caught me" grin at times. With Sallie and me he was not only polite, but actually affectionate. A few weeks after these events, O.J. turned eighteen. A girl on the other unit, who was enamored of our hero, baked him a birthday cake, which was very probably the first of his life. He consumed it all at one sitting, except for two pieces—one for me and one for Sallie. O.J. had dropped his guard for the first time in his life and started to let someone in, to let us see who he really was behind his ferocious and intimidating facade.

It turned out that O.J. was a remarkable young man. In fact, he was a natural poet, who spoke in visual images so striking you could see them in the air. O.J. used metaphor and imagery the way most folks use cliches and fad phrases. He didn't just tell a story, he painted it in your mind. He was a nice guy, too. By the time he left the unit he was unofficially a junior staff member, helping us to put the younger ones down for the night and keeping order with a mere glance or frown. I ran into him about a year later, driving down University again in my MG convertible. O.J. spotted me and flagged me down, pulling me over to meet his "partners," a couple of young men who were obviously pretty sure of their survival skills. I was a little edgy, but I trusted O.J. and was happy to see him. He greeted me like his old favorite coach, and his friends were respectful and friendly. O.J. was working regularly and basically supporting himself. He was a bad boy gone good.

What happened with O.J.? Why did our very simple interventions work? And what does his case tell us about what constitutes a "bad boy?" For me, O.J. is only the most graphic example of a general principle I've seen many times in my career. That is, that discipline is an act of love. All parental activities can be roughly categorized as either nurturing or discipline. Taking care of your kids, loving on 'em, cuddling and wrestling and playing ball and going to the zoo, is all nurturing. That's the fun part of parenting, the part that makes us feel good about ourselves and our children (though it also means getting up in the middle of the night, getting thrown up on, and spending money). Discipline means teaching kids to act right and be responsible. It means scolding, spanking, denying privileges, and rewarding good behavior. That's the hard part of parenting. In fact, discipline isn't fun, and the only reason you do it is that you love your kids and want them to turn out right. Like I said, it's equally an act of love. There's also the not wanting them to destroy your house, but that's another story.

Maybe that's why kids respond to fair, firm discipline not only with good behavior, but with affection. I've seen this reaction in kids from eighteen months to eighteen years of age. O.J. responded to Sallie and me by sharing his cake and then himself. Another "bad" teenager I'd caught red-handed in a lie met me at the door to the unit the next day with a hearty, "Yo, Catfish; what's happening, Dude?" (Referring to the handlebar mustache I then wore.) It was the first friendly word I'd heard from him. He'd actually looked on the duty roster to see when I came in, so he could greet me. With affection. The day before, he'd tried to run away and threatened me with a knife-sharp hair pick when I chased him down.

Later, at the Austin Child Guidance Center, I saw a fiery little nine-year-old who took offense at my explaining her manipulations and con artistry to her mother. She glared at me like a laser cannon and kicked me right smartly in the shin.

"Angel," I said, "this is my personal office and that's my personal leg you're kicking. If you try that again, I'll be forced to restrain you. Do you know what 'restrain' means?"

"Yeah, I know what it means," she snapped, and drew back to kick me again. This time I intercepted the blow, grabbed her legs and her hands, and held her tightly. We ended up on the floor with me holding her down, arms crossed, head pinned and legs immobile. I told her I would keep her under control until she could control herself, which she would indicate by five seconds of silence and utter lack of movement. It took her about half an hour to get still (Mom had long since bailed out), at which point I dried her eyes, gave her a hug, and sent her home. The next week she brought me a valentine saying, "I love you Dr. Bob." It was perhaps another con job, though certainly an improvement on her last efforts. But I truly believe she was sincere, as she and I got along very nicely from then on.

A divorced mother in Birmingham brought me her two-year-old son, who threw outrageous temper tantrums and "hated men." As I explained how to handle him, the toddler became bored and tried to exit the room. I told him no, and he began to scream and cry and kick at the door. I simply leaned on the door to keep it shut and proceeded to talk with the mother, completely ignoring the child. No, it wasn't easy, but I get a lot of practice. In a few minutes he got tired, grabbed one of my psychology books, and began leafing through it. I sat beside him and pointed to the few pictures in it, then got a children's book I thought he might prefer. We "read" it together a few minutes and he jumped up in my lap to see better. We finished the session quietly and without further incident. The next week he raced down the hallway and jumped into my arms. This kid didn't hate men; he merely disliked his mother's uncaring and neglectful boyfriends. As with O.J., Angel, and my young liar, this little boy needed discipline, and he responded to it with affection. I'm not denying that there are evil people in the world, but I think a lot of bad boys and girls simply lack discipline, which is to say love and understanding, along with firm limit-setting and enforcement of rules.

In my thirty-plus years of clinical practice, much of it with adolescents, I've had knives pulled on me, had kids swing at me, even faced a man with a rifle. Yet the only times I've actually been hit were by small children. The only time I ever got hurt—a few minor bruises—was in wrestling a wild teenager, in the process of strapping him to a hospital bed. He was very apologetic later and didn't hold my restraining him against me. He'd just been having a little too much fun, and he knew I was just doing my job. Even bad boys and girls can be capable of remarkable warmth and sympathy. One day in Group Therapy the kids noticed I wasn't my usual happy self and asked why. I revealed that my best friend had died the day before. The therapist isn't supposed to cry, but I couldn't help it at that point. And these dozen bad, crazy teenagers, all of them hospitalized for delinquency, drug abuse, suicide or psychosis, gathered me up in a group hug and comforted me. I don't think my credibility as a psychologist suffered any, and I was greatly moved by the love and humanity of these "bad," "mad" adolescents.

The sad truth is that good people do bad things sometimes. That's what we need forgiveness for. You never know what you might do in a given situation until you're actually in it. It's unwise to believe that a certain behavior is so uncharacteristic you couldn't possibly do it. As a psychologist I've seen all kinds of people do all kinds of things, including things they would not have believed themselves capable of. I've seen preachers have Internet affairs, mothers chain their children to the bed, husbands kill their wives and themselves. I've come to believe that almost anybody is capable of almost anything, given the right circumstances. Indeed, what makes many of these extraordinary actions so scary is that they were committed by very ordinary people. Many people, for example, believe themselves incapable of violence. Yet, I treated a little old gray-haired grandmother who'd been convicted of attempted murder and assault with a deadly weapon. She'd been verbally and physically abused by her husband for nearly forty years. He'd put her in the hospital several times, once to have her entire face rebuilt after he'd smashed it into the floorboards. One day he was indulging himself in a favorite pastime, sitting on their deck shooting past her head with a revolver. (They lived in the country, where no one could hear.) But she'd tired of this game and was no longer intimidated. She told him she was no longer scared of him and informed him, "I've got a gun, too." He laughed at her and went inside chuckling. That did it. She followed him into the bathroom with a .22 caliber pistol and put five bullets in him. He recovered after several months in the hospital, and they got divorced. She received a suspended sentence and five years' probation, as well as court-ordered therapy. She was a sweet, old-fashioned Southern lady who insisted on having me over for tea. The point is, if a sweet little gray-haired grandmother is capable of murder, who isn't?

Bad boys and girls need firm, consistent, responsible parents. Unfortunately, today's "bad" children often have either no parents or one over-worked and unavailable parent, or parents who are themselves highly conflicted and ambivalent about parenting. Today's parents are Baby-Boomers raised in the idealistic and romanticized post-war economic growth spurt. Raised on *Donna Reed, Leave It to Beaver,* and John Wayne movies, they were taught to idealize their parents, and authority in general, as all-loving, all-giving, all-knowing paragons of virtue and courage. Their fathers had won the war ("WWII, The Big One"), and their mothers created the perfect home and family. Then came the Vietnam War, in which American boys were conscripted to blow up villages and napalm children to support a corrupt right-wing dictator and stave off the nationalistic but left-wing aspirations of a popular folk hero. They were lied to by presidents and defense secretaries (one of whom admitted it in print). A president had to resign his office for criminal misconduct. The police, state troopers, and FBI used the force of government to suppress civil rights. Two popular presidents were exposed as having had affairs. No wonder the Boomers ended up with little faith in or respect for authority. Worse yet, many Boomer parents so thoroughly mistrust authority that they are often ambivalent and tentative about exercising their own. We've become "them." We're the bosses now, and we're very uncomfortable in the role. We want to love our kids, indulge them, help them to have good feelings about themselves. As a result, we've often failed to discipline, engendered a lot of phony and ephemeral self-esteem, ruined our educational system, and raised a generation of spoiled, ungrateful, rebellious, narcissistic children. Bad boys and girls. Mostly our fault; mostly their loss.

People have authority because they have a responsibility, a job to do. It wouldn't be right to have a responsibility and be held accountable for a job without having the authority to do it. Imagine yourself the supervisor in a production plant, charged with cranking out a million widgets a day. Yet you can't fire employees who slack off and under-produce, or give bonuses to those who knock themselves out and exceed their quotas. Your job depends on their production, yet you have no control over them. This is an unfair and highly undesirable place to be. That's why the supervisor has authority. For that matter, imagine you're the parent of a sixteen-year-old. If he steals a Mercedes and crashes it through somebody's living room, you get the bill. Yet, you have little control over him. You can't even put him in a treatment program without his consent. It's the law.

A policeman's responsibility is to maintain law and order. He can't do it if he hasn't the authority to tell you to "move along, there, Buddy." A teacher can't teach if she isn't allowed to maintain order in her class—which is what's happening across the country, as time-out, detention, and other disciplinary methods have been outlawed. Ironically, one result is that kids now get suspended for insignificant infractions because it's the only disciplinary means left. The parent's job is to raise an independent, self-reliant, moral, and responsible adult. You can't do that if you can't make and enforce rules with your kids. Here, too, we've seen how authority can be abused by mean, inebriated, or incompetent parents. Child abuse seems nearly epidemic. Yet we can't allow that danger to deter us from providing the firm, appropriate discipline our children require. Failing to discipline is failing to love. The end product is bad boys and girls.

There is, unfortunately, another group of bad kids and adults who are not misunderstood and who don't respond favorably to either discipline or psychotherapy. These are the sociopaths, and I've worked with loads of them. Once called "psychopaths" and now properly labeled "antisocial personalities," these are truly bad people. Sociopaths are users, takers, abusers, criminals, and con artists. They come in two main types: mean sons of bitches and charmers. "Mean s.o.b.'s" range from the schoolyard bully to the armed robber or rapist. They are interested only in their own pleasure, and they do not care how they get it. Other human beings are simply useful objects to these sociopaths. They will use and abuse them to get what they want, then discard them like Styrofoam popcorn. They are incapable of love and quite capable of violence. They do not feel guilt, do not have a conscience, and feel no remorse for their misdeeds. They are predators, emotionally fixated at the level of a T. rex, though they may be highly intelligent and clever. Many are sadistic, actually deriving sensual or sexual pleasure from inflicting pain. Others simply do not care about other human beings. For example, I saw an adolescent who'd shot and killed an elderly woman during a gang fight. The poor woman drove up to the curb, unaware of the conflict, and stood up with a bag of groceries, right into the line of fire. She was shot in the head. When I asked the young murderer how he felt about killing this innocent victim, his reply was that it was her fault. "She shouldn't have been there." Like other sociopaths, he had no sense of guilt or remorse. The very worst of these nearly constitute a sub-type of their own, the serial killers. These are the Ted Bundy, Jeffrey Dahmer, Charles Manson sort of killers, who are both truly psychotic (i.e., crazy) and truly psychopathic or evil. They are spectacular but rare. I try to avoid them as patients—or friends.

Less-mean s.o.b.'s are much more common and may be met anywhere. Some are outright crooks; some are unscrupulous businessmen; some are cops who've found they can be mean with impunity if they work the outside of the jail cells. This group overlaps significantly with narcissists, crack-heads, and petty criminals of all sorts. Every redneck honky-tonk is full of them, but so is every large corporation or police force. They can be dangerous, but more often they're just annoying and expensive. You can't avoid them all, but it's sure useful to recognize them quickly, minimize your losses, and move on. And for God's sake, don't marry one.

"Charmers" are also sociopaths and can do a lot of damage, but they typically aren't violent. They have more sophisticated, more civilized ways of using and hurting people. These are antisocial, but highly sociable, con artists. And they're *everywhere*. These are the unscrupulous salesmen, sleazy lawyers, corrupt politicians, and lying televangelists who prey on the rest of society—but do it *nicely*. These are the oily morticians who take advantage of bereaved loved ones and the unethical therapists who have sex with their vulnerable patients. These are also predators, but they abuse people nicely, not nastily. They are smooth, attractive, and often bright. They are charmers, and many of them never get caught or at least manage to play the system well enough not to get punished. The really good ones can still make you like them even when you know they're lying and cheating you. They are ultimately narcissistic.

One of my personal favorites I'll call "Alvin," since his cute little fat cheeks made him look like a chipmunk. I treated Alvin first at Hill Crest's Adolescent Unit, but he and his family drifted in and out of my practice for ten years, mostly in crisis. Alvin was seventeen when I first saw him, a tall, lean adolescent with buzz-cut hair, chubby cheeks, and very sincere-looking blue eyes. The honest eyes were just one of many ways Alvin would prove to be deceptive.

We got Alvin because he was suicidally depressed. He, his two brothers, and mother were living in poverty, having run away from a highly abusive father. Alvin's father was incredibly strong, a riveter who could run a riveting gun or jack-hammer up over his head all day long. Alvin had seen him literally throw his mother across a room, then slam-dunk her onto a glass table. He himself had been pinned to the wall by the throat, feet dangling a yard high, as his father described what he'd do if Alvin told the police on him. His little brothers actually soiled themselves in fear. So Alvin had good reasons to be anxious and depressed. Further, sixteen years of being called a "worthless little turd" had certainly tarnished Alvin's self-image. Alvin's dad was one mean s.o.b.

But Alvin had also inherited some of his old man's sociopathy, and his response to this dysfunctional family was characteristically narcissistic. He determined he was better than all this, and he'd prove it by becoming rich and famous—which he'd do by being a crook.

Actually, Alvin made several attempts to make it on the up and up. He somehow got himself a G.E.D., despite a poor education and a marginal IQ, and he landed a position as an apprentice mortician. I thought this a questionable career move, but Alvin was captivated with the intricacies and subtleties of the mortuary arts. He reveled in the macabre details of embalming techniques and facial reconstructions and was enthralled by the lugubrious art of selling over-priced casketry. Undertaking appealed to Alvin's long-repressed hostility and placed him in the company of vulnerable people with money. He was right; this could be his ticket to wealth and success.

To Alvin success meant owning a Jaguar automobile and a Rolex watch. Alvin had the self-esteem of a sea slug. He'd been abused and demeaned all his life, and humiliated by his helplessness as his father hammered his adored, if also slightly sociopathic, mother. He thought of himself as a born loser, a total jerk. But a British sports car and a Swiss watch would fix all that. He'd be a winner, a prince, a cool stud. His mother supplied the Jaguar, more or less, by moving the family in with a sleazy evangelistic "Jew for Jesus." Alvin saw through this opportunistic con artist at once, but he was happy enough with the new digs and delighted to recline on the Corinthian leather seats of the XJ-6. Meanwhile, he acquired the Rolex on his own. Or so he thought.

This was long after his release from the hospital, following a couple of minor disagreements with the local gendarmerie over a matter of questionably "found" stereos and VCRs. This followed another depression or two, a few bouts with the bottle, and a young lady in a possibly delicate condition out in Texas. Alvin showed up at my office flashing a Gold President Rolex, a watch then valued at over ten thousand dollars. He was very proud. I was very suspicious. How had this nearly destitute nineteen-year-old, employed as a grave-digger's gopher, acquired this fine European chronometer? His account of his good fortune was hardly reassuring. He'd befriended an aggrieved widow, he said, nurturing and supporting her through the death and entombment of her beloved, and wealthy, husband. In gratitude she'd given Alvin the watch, figuring it would serve him better than her late spouse.

It was almost believable. After all, Alvin had cute little dimples and fat little cheeks and honest blue eyes and a smile that could charm the Blarney right off the Stone. But I didn't buy it. Call me a cynic, or call me knowledgeable, or chalk it up to intuition or luck. I just didn't see a loving wife donating her late husband's prized timepiece to a smooth-talking kid. I got it out of him when the watch quit running and couldn't be fixed. Under intense interrogation Alvin confessed that he'd actually bought the watch from a rather shady street vendor. He'd paid $300, a fabulous bargain, even for a very toasty piece of wrist candy. I pressed on, and under extreme duress Alvin admitted the Rolex Gold President was actually an Oriental counterfeit, a piece of fool's gold worth no more than fifty bucks. There's no con easier to con than another con. He who lives by deceit dies by deceit.

I was happy to see Alvin take his show on a road tour. I was seeing several MPDs (patients with multiple personality disorder) by this time, and boredom was not a major career problem for me. But Alvin did reappear occasionally and always in an interesting fashion. Probably the best was his fling with the daughter of a Houston oil baron. Alvin loved his Calvin Klein wardrobe and Gucci luggage and Movado watches. He may have loved the daughter, though I have my doubts. He didn't like her father recalling his "borrowed" Gold Card and insisting on repayment or incarceration. I brokered a reimbursement and rehabil-itation deal, arguing Alvin suffered from a bipolar disorder (formerly called manic-depressive illness). Alvin was happy, but I'm not sure I served society's best interests in the transaction.

I didn't see Alvin for several years after that, and I can't say my life was the worse for it. When he did resurface, he dropped in to tell me he was working, was married, and had two kids. He was doing well, was living responsibly, and was happy. I was glad to see it. Alvin was a con artist and a petty thief, but I always kind of liked him and recognized that he truly was a victim of childhood abuse and poor parenting. His mother was a professional victim and a better con artist than Alvin had ever been, and she had unlimited faith in my ability to extricate him from any jam he could get into. I thanked him for the visit and told him to "keep in touch."

The latest call came from Alvin's wife "Juno." She told me that Alvin was interred in the Walker County lockup, with a whole lot of folks unhappy about him writing checks on a not-actually-existing account. He was off his lithium and a little manic and a little suicidal and a whole lot wanting to get out of stir. I allowed I couldn't help much and referred him to the mental health center in Jasper. I figured I'd done my fair share over the years. Bad boys are sad characters who experience—and cause—a great deal of sorrow. They're also just plain bad. And they're slow learners. Poor Alvin has spent most of his life trying to overcome a bad self-image by decorating himself with fancy watches and cars. He's never figured out that if you act like a jerk, acquiring a fine British sports car won't help much. It just makes you a jerk in a Jag.

I've seen a few bad girls, too, one of whom showed me just how determined some people are to rebel. "Anna" wasn't evil or mean or sociopathic, but she did not like to follow the rules. A slender, long-haired beauty of fourteen, she was a sweet and friendly child, but she couldn't seem to get home on time, be where she was supposed to be, turn in her homework, or resist the impulse to explain to her teachers how pathetically misguided they were.

She was a fairly typical fourteen-year-old who finds herself possessed of limitless knowledge, while surrounded by moronic adults set on advising and controlling her. She owed it not only to herself, but to the good of all humanity to resist. So Anna resisted and rebelled like a teenaged Trotskyite. Her parents were accustomed to the old, docile, compliant Anna, and this new revolutionary had them completely baffled. They tried all the usual parent stuff, but Anna was really tenacious, and nothing had much impact. Anna's grades continued to drop, and she managed to get herself suspended from school with a dreary regularity, mostly for talking out of turn or failing to arrive at class before the bell did. There were also some pretty creative cafeteria stunts primarily featuring Jello. I tried my psychological stuff, but I wasn't doing a lot better than her folks. Her delinquency was minor but persistent; she was truly dedicated.

Then Anna's case took a dramatic and lethal detour. Her parents came in one week without her, explaining that her allergies were acting up and she was home in bed. It was a good chance to plot our strategies behind her back, so we did a parent consult and went on home. Anna didn't make it the next week either. Her allergies were apparently worse and she complained of bad sinus headaches. She'd only been to school two days and had returned early from one of them. Decongestants and antihistamines weren't helping much, and they had a doctor's appointment in a couple of days. When Anna failed her third session I began to be concerned. Further, Anna's parents described her as increasingly lethargic and apathetic, mostly sleeping, barely eating, and clearly not making any progress. Her pediatrician had been consulted by phone but didn't feel he needed to see her. She'd be better in a few days. He'd prescribed no new medications. I told her parents to call me the next day and talked with the psychiatrist at the Clinic.

Dad called, as requested, and told me Anna was barely responsive. All he could get in her was a sip of beer, and he'd had to slap her face to arouse her enough for that. I told him to bring her in at once and talked to my doc. When they got her to the mental health center Anna was nearly comatose. My psychiatrist friend took one look at her and told me to get her to the emergency room *stat*. She called the hospital and got a neurosurgeon to the ER while I carried Anna to my ancient Jaguar and headed downtown. They took her into surgery immediately and opened her skull. Her sinus infection, untreated, had abscessed into her brain. The neurosurgeon told me she'd never wake up, and if she did she'd be a hopeless "veggie." (Doctors *do* use this term.) There was no chance of recovery. Her parents were devastated, and I was pretty distraught. Her pediatrician, if he had an ounce of sense (which he hadn't demonstrated so far), was consulting his lawyer.

Three weeks later Anna walked into my office, wrapped in a blanket and with considerable assistance, but on her own feet. She was weak, but quite lucid and in remarkably good spirits. I'm not much of a believer in miracles, but the word fits well here. In three more weeks she was back in school, and a week after that she was suspended for talking back to a teacher. We almost cheered. Anna was back!

Anna never was all that bad, and she eventually settled down and grew up. By now I suspect she's a lovely, loving mother with teenagers of her own. But if Anna still wanted to be bad, I'd pity the husband who tried to stop her. A brain abscess couldn't do it.

CHAPTER THREE

Ritalin and the Red Riveter

ATTENTION DEFICIT DISORDER, WITH AND without Hyperactivity (ADD or ADHD), has been a mainstay of my practice for nearly forty years. It's not a particularly sexy disorder, and it continues to be awash in a flood of controversy. Its sufferers are sometimes annoying, even dangerous characters, who can be quite difficult to manage. But ADHD is meat and potatoes to me.

My first acquaintance with ADHD was at PACE, a residential treatment program for adolescents. Having been trained at the University of Illinois, a bastion of behavior modification, I did not believe in a "medical" condition as the cause of misbehavior. Nor did I favor the use of medication. Behavior modification was the treatment of choice for all problems. Cognition, emotion, and physiology could safely be ignored; only behavior was important. But then I met "The Red Riveter," a hyperactive thirteen-year-old, who forced me to discard my over-stated theories and look more closely at practical realities.

His real name was Joey, but he styled himself "The Red Riveter" because he was red-headed and so hyper he was on you constantly, "like a riveting gun." Joey wasn't a mean kid, just a mischievous one. He was always into something, whether sneaking into the TV room at midnight, short-sheeting someone's bed, or stealing the teacher's magic markers (which he used as an inhalant to get "high"). And Joey was annoying, Guinness-book annoying. He was constantly pushing limits, trying to manipulate, or simply "bugging" you. It was his favorite sport. The other kids were constantly swatting him, and the staff would have if they could. Joey was so annoying that no teacher would flunk him, because in his small school, with only one class per grade, she'd have him again the next year. Every year Joey was promoted to become some other teacher's tormentor. That's why no one had discovered, in eight years of schooling, that Joey was totally illiterate. He could not read or write anything but his own name.

At PACE Joey was thoroughly evaluated and found to be severely dyslexic. An optometry consult indicated his eyes focused on two lines of print at once. No wonder he couldn't read. A pair of special glasses solved that problem, and Joey learned to read fluently in just a few weeks. His ping-pong game also improved dramatically, although he was already pretty good. We also found that he was very bright, which was how he'd faked his way through elementary school and why he was such a good con artist. Finally, he proved to have a serious attention deficit with hyperactivity to burn.

Joey was short in stature, as many ADHD patients are, but he was possessed of a "cyclonic" activity level. As with William, I found Joey easiest to relate to across a ping-pong table, though it could hardly be called "therapy." Playing my best all-around game I could usually take him, but Joey was the best purely defensive player I ever saw. He'd set me up with a huge lob, and I'd smash it as hard as I could. Joey'd race back twenty feet or more, scoop it up and serve me up another fat mush ball to slam. Eventually I'd miss one, but Joey never did. And he was so fast he could scamper back to the net if I tried to surprise him with a dink drop shot. I couldn't penetrate his consistent defense.

Meanwhile, Joey's behavior therapy was producing zero results. There too, we couldn't penetrate his defenses. At PACE we had as nearly total control over our patients as it is possible to have. They were locked in and dependent on us for all their needs. Each child was on an individualized behavior program. Everything he did or didn't do either earned or lost tokens, and tokens were required for everything from a hot meal to a warm bed. We received a daily print-out on each kid, telling us what behaviors he was displaying, and we could alter his program at will. The staff were highly trained and there were lots of them. It was a model program, beautifully designed and efficiently managed. If ever a behavior modification program was going to work, PACE would be it. And for most kids it did work—our average length of stay was about three months, with similar programs hitting around six or seven. With Joey, it accomplished nothing, except perhaps to harden his resolve to rebel. Joey was going on six months and still at the "freshman" level. Clearly a new strategy was indicated.

Much to our distaste, we were forced to turn to Ritalin, the new wonder drug of the day. We didn't alter Joey's behavior program at all; we just added the medication. His improvement was immediate and dramatic. Suddenly he began earning all his tokens. He'd always known what he was supposed to do, but now for the first time, he did it. In three weeks, the minimum possible time, Joey worked his way to sophomore, to junior, to senior, then graduated and went home. We were both pleased and chagrined. We'd found a potent therapeutic tool which could obviously benefit other patients as well. Yet it wasn't our cherished behavior therapy.

Ritalin was and is a controversial medicine. Although categorized as a Class II narcotic, it's not a tranquilizer or sedative at all. In fact it is chemically a close kin to the amphetamines. Its first cousins Dexedrine and Adderall are dextro-amphetamine, which is to say, "speed." Is it ethical to give such a potent drug to children? Is it right to control behavior chemically? And what paradoxical mumbo-jumbo uses *speed* to calm a hyperactive child? The controversy continues, partly due to unfair, even deceitful attacks by groups that that oppose nearly all med- ications. Many people honestly feel Ritalin is greatly over-prescribed and used as a crutch or an artificial booster to launch mediocre stu- dents to the heights of academe. On the other hand, there is no doubt that Ritalin and its related drugs Dexedrine and Adderall have the best therapeutic results of any form of treatment for ADHD, especially when combined with family counseling and our old friend "behav- ior mod." And there's a certain degree of built-in protection against over-prescription: with "normal" kids it not only won't help much, but it probably will make them "speedy."

We still don't understand ADHD all that well, but we're getting better. There's pretty compelling evidence that it is genetic and involves the *under*-functioning of brain cells in the prefrontal cortex. This is where the brain's inhibitory and focusing centers are primarily located. The core problem seems to be a failure of impulse control, including the impulse to shift one's attention too quickly. The stimulant medications seem to boost the activity of cells in these control centers, giving the patient nearly normal control of inhibitory mechanisms. Now he can maintain his focus and resist impulses to steal, lie, hit people, or talk out in English class. I treated Joey in 1970, and in 2015 I still don't like using Ritalin. But I've recommended it and its cousins to many hundreds of patients, and I'll continue to do so until something better comes along. When it works as intended, it's the closest thing to magic you'll ever see. In fact, I question the ethics of *not* prescribing stimulant medication for a child with ADHD who is failing academically, in constant trouble, and whose self-esteem suffers from continued failure, criticism, and punishment.

If Ritalin is over-prescribed, it may be partly due to misdiagnosis. There are many conditions that can produce a clinical syndrome strongly resembling ADHD, but which do not typically respond well to stimulant medication. This is mostly because they involve cells that are damaged or absent, rather than underfunctioning. Lead poisoning and brain trauma are good examples. One of the meanest kids I ever saw is another. "Poncho" was a well-developed four-year-old I treated in Austin. The first time I laid eyes on him, Poncho stormed across my office and began pummeling me viciously, arms flailing and eyes flashing wildly. This kid could have kick-boxed with Bruce Lee or Jackie Chan. It was pretty quickly obvious that behavior therapy wasn't going to get anywhere with this wild man. Reluctantly, the staff psychiatrist and I agreed to try Ritalin, a somewhat questionable move in a patient so young. But this kid was out of control, and we needed help. To our dismay, Ritalin made him even worse. On a hunch, Dr. Ceballos put him on Benadryl, an antihistamine used to combat allergies. It settled Poncho down at once, revealing the bright, good-natured child he should have been. A pediatric allergist confirmed that Poncho was allergic to everything in the known universe, probably up to and including Einsteinium. Poncho was hyper and aggressive and impulsive and unfocused, not because he had ADHD, but because he felt *awful*.

I've also seen "ADHD" patients who turned out to be mentally retarded, psychotic, or learning disabled. ADD/ADHD is not a simple diagnosis and should not be made without appropriate evaluation, to include at least an IQ test and parent and teacher checklists. Unfortunately, managed care typically won't pay for psychological testing. (I don't mean to run a vendetta on managed care companies; in fact, I used to do case reviews for one. And I understand that their contracts do not allow for unlimited therapy, etc. Still, it's an unfortunate situation.) Thus, many therapists and physicians are forced to diagnose and treat what may be ADHD on the basis of a single diagnostic interview or the parents' unsubstantiated report. The result is that they use Ritalin diagnostically: if it helps, the child is presumed to have ADHD, and vice versa. This is poor practice, if not unethical, and it's a short-sighted way to save a few bucks. This is especially true when the evaluation may also pick up on co-morbid conditions of learning disability, depression, or oppositional-defiant disorder, all of which are common in ADHD patients.

Stimulant medication is not supposed to be used in children under six, but I've recommended it for kids as young as three and a half. I had a three-and-a-half-year-old patient who'd been ejected from twelve of the thirteen day care centers in his town, and he *had* to be in day care. Ritalin saved his academic career and his mother's job as well. The stimulants have been said to have a "paradoxical" calming effect in children, the reverse of its adult action. In fact, they work exactly the same for both, producing an apparent calmness by allowing the patient to concentrate. Adderall saved the career of an adult patient who was on the verge of being dismissed from his Residency in family medicine, which points to another myth—that you outgrow ADHD. Unfortunately, you do not, and many adults continue to suffer from it. Adults with ADD do tend to be less "hyper," but many continue to be impulsive and inattentive. Adults have the advantage of mostly being able to choose what they attend to, a luxury denied to children and adolescents. Thus, attending may not be a problem, as they choose careers they find interesting and engaging.

This can change, too, of course, and what was not a problem can become one. For example, a man whose son was on Dexedrine consulted me about his own attention problem. He was a mechanical engineer, a design specialist who was involved in creating new widgets for his company to manufacture. He'd work at his computer or drawing table, run down to the Line to see if it could be machined, talk to the marketing boys about whether it would sell, then trot over to Accounting to determine its profitability. He loved his job and he was good at it, so good they promoted him to head up Research and Development. Now instead of moving at will throughout the plant he was confined to a desk eight hours a day, reading and reviewing other people's design proposals. He was bored silly and could not make himself pay attention. He was drinking thirty cups of coffee a day, each cup providing two excuses to get up (one to fetch and one to pee), and each containing caffeine, a mild stimulant related to the amphetamines. His ADD had not troubled him as a design engineer, but it was a major hindrance to his management position.

There are many people who still question whether ADHD should be considered a "disorder" at all. After all, the syndrome consists of traits found in the normal population (inattention, impulsivity, hyperactivity) and exists in about 7 percent of all people. If it's such a disorder, why does it persist in the gene pool? Perhaps it's because ADHD is a positive asset in some situations. Being quick to decide and to move may save your life in the jungle. You and I meet a Bengal tiger wandering about the jungle. You impulsively haul butt. I stop to think about the situation, figure out "where the tiger is coming from," maybe try to negotiate or help the tiger meet his needs in alternative ways. You're gone, I'm lunch. ADHD is also useful at times in the jungle of the business world.

Studies have found the rate of ADHD to be as high as 25 percent in a group of *successful* entrepreneurs. However, ADHD is certainly not an asset in a history class. And doubters are welcome to spend a weekend with the Red Riveter; he'll make believers out of them.

For those who do suffer from ADHD it can be a surprisingly pervasive problem, showing up in diverse areas of their lives, far removed from the classroom. I've seen a couple who divorced because she could no longer tolerate his annoying ADHD habits. He didn't listen to her, a frequent wife's complaint, but in his case clearly exacerbated by his ADHD inattentiveness. He procrastinated terribly, failing to give the kids their lunch money, failing to renew his insurance policy, paying taxes late, etc. She interpreted this as passive-aggressive, and some of it probably was. In any case, she wanted out, at least temporarily. ADHD is also behind many peoples' over-reactive emotionality, especially their anger. The story of "Hondo" is illustrative.

Hondo was a lanky, good-looking, foul-tempered sixteen-year-old. He was incredibly impulsive (the hallmark of ADHD) and had an explosive temper he was unable to control. I worked with him at Hill Crest Hospital during my brief tenure as Director of the Adolescent Unit. Hondo got sent to us after a confrontation with his father. He'd gotten so angry he'd been afraid he'd assault his dad, which he knew to be inadvisable. Dad was blocking the only exit and he knew he had to get out, so he did—right through a plate glass window. Hondo's temper was legendary, as was his skill at fisticuffs. Hondo was the best fighter in his school, by acclamation. Anyone seeking to enhance his own reputation did so by challenging Hondo. Even a respectable loss would earn increased respect. Hondo was usually quite willing to oblige, but if he happened to lack interest it was easy to get him angry enough to fight anyway. He'd been suspended so many times he by-passed the principal's office and simply headed home after each new bout. He had plenty of takers, even though he never lost. Lasting two minutes with Hondo would automatically put you on the Middleweight contenders' list. Five minutes would probably earn a shot at the Title, but nobody ever got far enough to find out.

Hondo was growing tired of all this and was ready to grow up. He didn't really like being suspended and he hated the hospital. Even the fighting itself was getting boring, as he never lost. He wanted to quit and he knew that meant controlling his temper. Prozac (an anti-depressant that also seems to help with angry moods) helped a bit, but it wasn't enough. So Hondo and I studied anger management techniques. He learned to control his temper by thinking more rationally and functionally. He learned to think, "Gee, that's annoying" instead of, "That's awful and I can't stand it!" He learned not to tell himself that he had to respond to all taunts, jokes, or challenges and to think instead, "It's really my own self-respect I need, and I can't have that if I allow myself to lose my cool."

Hondo was a good student and he developed amazing self-control. When he returned to school he announced his retirement from the fight game; he was hanging up his gloves. Naturally, everyone was shocked, but they all seemed to respect his decision, even if they doubted his ability to stick with it. All, that is, except one aspiring young punk who thought he'd discovered a fast way to glory. This Bad Boy confronted Hondo in the hall, blocking his way and getting right "in his face."

"I'm the baddest kid in this school, and I'm gonna kick your ass to prove it," he declared.

"I'm sure you are," said Hondo, "except I don't fight anymore. You'll have to prove it with somebody else." Hondo tried to walk around the boy, but again he was blocked.

"You'll fight," said the punk. "I'll make you." And he delivered a quick right jab to Hondo's jaw. Hondo was no sucker and he rolled with the punch, but still took a bit of a shot. By this time a considerable crowd had gathered, eager to witness the demise of this brash and intemperate challenger. They knew Hondo would kill him. But Hondo continued to decline the invitation. The Bad Boy insisted he would, but Hondo simply stated that he would not fight, but he would visit the principal's office and have his assailant thrown out of school. Bad Boy threw a huge roundhouse blow and Hondo took it with little more than a shrug. He'd taken two clean licks and barely batted an eye.

"Are you done, yet?" he asked calmly.

"I guess I am," the punk admitted.

"Then I believe I'll keep my promise and get your butt tossed out," said Hondo, and he did. After this incident Hondo's reputation as a tough guy was better than ever. He'd gained more prestige for *not* fighting than for jumping on the least provocation.

I asked Hondo how he'd done it. "I changed my thinking, Coach, just like we talked about." Which illustrates something else about ADHD and its treatment. Medication alone is not enough. Behavior therapy and sometimes counseling and family therapy are also required. In Hondo's case rational behavior therapy, plus a little Prozac, may well keep him out prison, which is filled with untreated people with ADHD.

Children with ADHD get yelled at and punished a lot because they tend to act on impulse, making their behavior poorly thought out and often inappropriate. They do poorly in school because they cannot force themselves to sit still and pay attention. They may be rejected by their peers, since even kids find pushy, hyperactive, overly emotional kids annoying. Thus, they grow up thinking of themselves as bad, stupid, and unlovable. By the time I see them, the primary ADHD symptoms, which are generally treatable with medication, may not even be the major problem. We often spend more time on self-esteem and relationship issues, which, of course, requires good old psychotherapy.

Of course, it still takes Ritalin to keep them on the "couch" long enough to learn anything.

CHAPTER FOUR

Touched by God, or "The Fear of the Lord"

ONE OF MY FIRST OFFICE (not hospital) patients was a gloomy, frumpy middle-aged teacher named Mildred. I was a graduate student at Illinois, and I saw Mildred as a part of a practicum in systematic desensitization. This technique was pioneered by one of my professors and consisted of slowly unlearning phobic responses by very relaxed and gradual exposure to the feared object. But Mildred was no simple phobic, though it took a six-month battle to convince her of that. Even as a rank amateur (though with two years of residential treatment experience) it was clear to me that Mildred was suffering from a much more severe anxiety disorder. Her "contamination phobia" was only part of a classic obsessive-compulsive disorder. But let's ease into Mildred's story by detouring through a brief examination of the simple phobias. It'll help make OCD more understandable.

My other main patient in that practicum was a second generation Greek immigrant named Kristina. For me she will always be "The Bird Lady." She did have a simple phobia and was an appropriate candidate for desensitization, although her case illustrates how complex even "simple" phobias can become. Kristina was afraid of birds. She'd been attacked and mauled by a rooster as a young girl and had been pretty well traumatized. He'd pecked and clawed her up pretty badly and had gotten tangled in her long, black hair, beating his wings against her face. From then on, she was terrified of roosters, and by the time I saw her, in her fifties, her phobia had generalized to *all* birds. She went to great lengths to avoid exposure to birds, especially birds not in cages. Now this doesn't sound too incapacitating, as Kristina lived in the city, but her phobia had come to dominate and control her whole life. Indeed, she could talk of little else, which was driving her husband crazy as well. Kristina was afraid to attend services at her Greek Orthodox church because its elaborate Neo-Byzantine stonework harbored the roosts of hundreds of pigeons. (Actually, there's an element of reality to this fear, as anyone who's ever been dive-bombed by a pigeon can attest; but that's another story.) She loved the park, but it had all kinds of birds, including plenty of picnic-mooching pigeons who walked right up to you. Kristina was an avid golfer, but the fifteenth fairway had a large water hazard/duck pond she could not play around. She was unable to shop at Sears, once her favorite department store, because in those days they had a pet department, which included canaries, parakeets, and cockatiels. She couldn't even visit a friend without calling first to see if they had a pet bird and if so was it in a cage, was the cage locked securely, and so on. She got a lot of attention for her phobia, which probably helped to maintain it, but Kristina's life was a mess, all because of an irrational (mostly, even to her) fear of birds.

So we set to work desensitizing her, first teaching her to relax herself physically, then proceeding step by step through gradually closer exposure to birds, first merely in her imagination, then in real-life trials. The idea is that by remaining calm in the presence of the phobic object one gradually overcomes one's fear, one tiny step at a time. It's a tedious process and as boring as white bread for the therapist, but it does work. I also removed the "secondary gain" of attention by denying her permission to talk about birds with anyone but me. Her husband was immensely grateful.

Kristina was gradually getting better. Together we had conquered Sears and had her playing all but the fifteenth hole. Friends' houses were now safe for her. Then she had a real breakthrough entirely on her own. Kristina lived in Decatur, Illinois, where not even the constant roasting of soybeans could dispel the frigid winds roaring across the flatlands from Canada. Kristina, on assignment from me, went to the park to visit the ducks, and there she met with a disturbing sight. The pond was entirely frozen over, and the poor ducks had no food, no water, and no friendly keeper to care for them. A good-hearted and generous soul, Kristina was distraught, and she ran to the store, bought a huge bag of popcorn, and, swallowing her fear, stepped out of the car to feed the ducks. She quickly tossed a handful of popcorn to one side, and the ducks made a frantic scramble to retrieve it. She tossed another handful in the other direction, and mallard mania broke loose again, as they climbed over each other, quacking and squawking furiously. Two things happened to Kristina. First, she recognized that she had some control over the situation, as she could direct the ducks by selective popcorn tossing. That made her feel less fearful, as a sense of mastery or control usually reduces people's level of anxiety. Second, she couldn't help noticing that the waddling, squabbling ducks made a hilarious show. At that realization her fear disappeared entirely. You don't fear what you find comical. The last I saw of her Kristina was heading up a Friends of the Ducks committee to improve conditions at the zoo and was much too busy to worry about any silly old phobias.

Kristina provides a nice example of how simple phobias work. They often begin with a real childhood trauma, tend to generalize to other similar stimuli, and can lead to avoidance patterns which dominate and greatly inconvenience one's life. They may produce "secondary gain," real-life advantages such as attention or controlling others, which help to maintain them. They respond well to behavior therapy which involves controlled, gradual exposure to the feared object. Actually, there is another way to rid yourself of the phobia, and that is to overwhelm oneself with sudden, massive exposure to the feared object. You will be terrified at first, but how long can you continue to be scared to death when you don't actually die? You can oonch gradually into the baby end of the pool or plunge into the deep end, but you can't overcome your fear of the water without actually getting wet. That's one reason the "Problem of Avoidance" is so destructive: it effectively eliminates any opportunity to overcome the phobia, because the phobic object is never confronted. And the avoidance behaviors themselves can take enormous time and energy, which is the other half of the Problem of Avoidance. Another patient had a panic attack while crossing over the Mississippi River Bridge at Vicksburg. A panic attack is essentially the inappropriate activation of the primitive "fight or flight" response. One's body is preparing to run away from or to fight a tiger, in order to save oneself from becoming cat food. You start hyperventilating, your heart rate soars, you feel warm all over, and you can't think clearly. You may even throw up. All these are normal and very useful in maximizing blood flow to your muscles, which is essential for whupping up on or escaping from the tiger. Not very useful in four lanes of fast-moving traffic on a mile-long bridge with no place to pull over. So he developed a phobia to that bridge. Fine, so he can cross the Big Muddy at Baton Rouge or Memphis. But phobias tend to spread to other, similar objects, then to less similar ones. He became fearful of all big bridges, then ALL bridges. His subsequent avoidance of bridges had him driving fifty miles out of the way to avoid even so much as a culvert. He couldn't visit his grandmother, because she lived off a country highway, and her driveway crossed the drainage ditch by way of a culvert—to him a "bridge." Interstates were all out of the question for him, as they are really a series of ramps and overpasses. Ironically, bridges were causing him no harm, but avoidance of them was ruining his entire life. I had him start with the culvert, driving very slowly and practicing the relaxation skills I taught him, recrossing until he was bored silly. Then do the same with a very slightly larger bridge, and so on (systematic desensitization). It worked.

Unfortunately, simple phobias are rarely the presenting problem for psychotherapy. Anxious people typically have other anxiety problems as well. Much more common, in my clinical experience, is Obsessive Compulsive Disorder, or OCD, an anxiety disorder of much greater magnitude and much harder to treat. Mildred, my other practicum patient, had OCD in a big way.

In OCD the patient experiences recurrent, intrusive thoughts, which he or she recognizes as alien, irrational, undesirable, and disturbing, but which cannot be expelled from consciousness. The thoughts make her anxious, but she can't stop thinking them. Only by acting out some ritual can she temporarily rid herself of them. For example, the obsessive thought might be, "I wonder if I left the stove turned on; it could start a fire." The compulsive ritual is to go check the stove—often a magical, specific number of times—to be *sure* the stove is off. Acting out the ritual reduces the anxiety, and this is rewarding, so the behavior of checking is automatically reinforced or strengthened, making it ever more likely to recur. And since you can't *not* think the intrusive thought, and you get terribly anxious without performing the ritual, the obsessive-compulsive is stuck in a self-perpetuating cycle. OCD may have genetic or other biological underpinnings and often responds well to medication, but it also involves a cognitive error, the search for absolute certainty in a probabilistic universe. We inhabit a universe in which motion and the thing which is moving are just different forms of the same thing. Matter and energy are equivalent. We live in a universe in which chunks and squiggles are indistinguishable, and light can appear as either a fluid wave or a solid hunk, depending on how you look at it. In our universe seemingly empty space is alive with frantic motion, "solid" objects are made up mostly of nothing, and subatomic particles come willy-nilly in and out of existence at their own discretion. In such a universe, and with our growing scientific awareness that human memory is notoriously subject to error and alteration, how can anybody ever be *sure* of *anything*? Do I remember checking the stove today, or is that really a memory from last month, or do I only remember *imagining* that I checked it? How can I be truly certain? The answer, of course, is that I can't. I can only know with a certain level of probability that something may or may not have happened. But the obsessive-compulsive isn't comfortable with that; he wants to know for *sure*. And so he resorts to magical thinking and magical rituals to dispel his doubts and the anxiety that accompanies them.

Mildred was a schoolteacher in her mid-forties, never married, and still living with her mother and sister. She was solidly built, but not fat, plain, but not ugly, and had once been honored as Teacher of the Year for the State of Illinois. I started seeing her in icy January, but it was well into temperate May before I saw her without gloves and tightly buttoned overcoat, which remained on throughout our sessions. She was courteous, bright, articulate, strong-willed, and unhappy. A devout Roman Catholic, Mildred was obsessed with the fear of being "contaminated" by minute particles of the Communion wafer or "Host." A deeply religious woman, Mildred was tragically, ironically, deathly afraid of being touched by—God.

In the Catholic faith, in which I myself was raised, the unleavened bread of the Eucharist, the Communion Host, is considered to be the true, literal, actual body and blood of Jesus Christ. Not a symbol, not just a remembrance, but the real thing. Thus, the host is worthy of great respect, and it is a grievous sin to desecrate it by intentionally showing disrespect or disregard for it. Purposely stepping on the host or throwing it aside would be a desecration and therefore a mortal sin. Thus, the church has for centuries provided altar boys with a clean brass plate to hold under the chins of communicants lest a particle of the host fall to the floor accidentally and be trodden upon like any common breadcrumb.

Mildred, a fearful and secretly angry woman, began to be afraid that she would somehow desecrate the communion host. She began to take precautions against this frightening prospect, which could land her a permanent suite in the nether regions, the land *way* down under. She first was extremely careful at communion, then declined to go at all, moved to the rear of the church, and finally quit attending mass altogether. But her obsession with contamination grew and with it her compulsive, ritualistic acting-out. *Any* contact with the Host at all was potentially a desecration, and Mildred began to consider ways in which she might accidentally, even unknowingly, come to be touched by particles of the host. This fear gradually took the form of a classic "contamination phobia." She became obsessed with the thought of contamination by particles which she fervently believed to be the real body and blood of her God. Her ritualistic precautions became ever more elaborate, and she could not stop imagining ways in which she could become contaminated, requiring ever more compulsive avoidance and cleansing rituals. Her obsessive-compulsive disorder blossomed and grew until it dominated her every thought and action. She came to see me because she could no longer force herself to touch her students' papers, and her job was in jeopardy. She could not tolerate her students handing her their papers. Instead she had them place the papers on her desk, where she could collect them later—with gloves on. The students were beginning to talk.

Once something had become "contaminated" in Mildred's thinking, it was contaminated forever. She had come to take elaborate precautions against contamination, such as wearing gloves and coats everywhere. But once used, they were themselves contaminated and could not be touched again. It was the same with purses. Mildred owned closets full of coats, chests full of gloves, and attics full of barely used, but permanently untouchable clothing and accessories. This was why she kept her coat buttoned in my office well into May and discarded her gloves only after five months of therapy. Being obsessive and highly intelligent, she couldn't stop thinking up new ways she might be contaminated, and she realized that she would eventually contaminate the entire planet, leaving her no place left to stand. Before I met her this thought had driven her to a psychotic breakdown, and she'd been found weeping on the church floor, after a night of terror. Ironically, she'd been taken to the Psych unit at St. Vincent's, a Catholic hospital where priests regularly carried Communion to the patients.

Here's an example of how Mildred's OCD thinking led to life-stopping avoidance behavior: she'd stopped attending evening teachers' meetings for fear of contamination. Mildred reasoned that one of the teachers might be Catholic, might have attended morning Mass, might have gone to Communion, might have gotten particles of the host on her lips, might be a smoker, might have transferred particles from her lips to a cigarette, might have touched the cigarette and then an ash-tray, thereby transferring particles of the host to the ashtray at the meeting. Mildred might be called upon to pass the ashtray (this was back in acceptable smoking days) and thereby become contaminated herself. She knew this thinking was crazy, but the risk was just too high to take.

Mildred was not an easy case. The first task was to gain her trust and get her focused on the real problem. Looking back from the perspective of an experienced and presumably mature clinician, I can only marvel at the ability of this paranoid woman to extend her faith to an untried, hippie-garbed student with a handle-bar mustache and barely half her years. She was a good and a desperate woman. Mildred insisted her problem was a simple phobia and demanded desensitization, while I diagnosed her problem as OCD and recommended psychotherapy. (This was years before Prozac.) It was only with the assistance of my supervisor, a nationally recognized expert in treatment of phobias, that Mildred reluctantly abandoned her treatment plan and began to submit to mine. Finally forging a therapeutic alliance, we slowly found ways to beat back her OCD and begin to reclaim her life.

It helped that I was both logical and under-handed. I used Mildred's intelligence and faith to undermine her "phobia." Recalling my Catholic upbringing, I pointed out to her that taking excessive precautions against committing sacrilege was a sign of scrupulosity, and therefore was itself a sin of pride. This was true because it implied that one set for oneself a higher standard than God's. Just to be safe, I checked it out with her priest, and he backed me up entirely. This gave me a major weapon in our battle with OCD. I needed only to define what "excessive" meant; anything beyond that was scrupulous, prideful, sinful, and therefore not acceptable. At this point, Mildred's rationality and education became assets. She agreed to define "excessive" as "scientifically unrealistic and improbable." If some event was simply so utterly unlikely as to be beyond any realistic probability of occurring, it was illogical and excessive to take precautions against its occurrence. I knew I had her when she bought this line of reasoning, because the chain of events she imagined was about as likely as a Boston terrier becoming Pope. We reviewed probability theory and agreed that a one-in-a-million chance of desecration was the outer limit of "reasonable precautions." Math did the rest. You'll recall that the probability of two events both occurring is the probability of the first multiplied by the probability of the second. If there's a one-in-ten chance of Event A occurring and a one-in-ten chance of Event B, the chance of both A and B occurring is only one in a hundred. If Event C is fifty-fifty, then Events ABC all occurring is a one in two hundred probability. In a long chain of fairly unlikely events the numbers go up pretty fast. If one teacher in three is Catholic (realistic in her community) and one Catholic out of ten attends mass daily, and only one-fifth of these goes to Communion (back in the days when one had to fast completely, no food since midnight to go to Communion, which would leave one too weak to face a day of teaching tenth-graders), and only one in twenty gets particles on her lips, and only one third are smokers, and so on—then the chance of becoming "contaminated" by passing an ash-tray that night is only one in several billions. Refusing to attend meetings becomes a sin of pride. Score so far: mental health one, OCD zero.

We got some help from biology, too. The Catholic Church taught that the communion wafer continued to be the true body and blood of Christ only so long as it maintained the physical appearance and biological reality of bread. Once it decayed or was metabolized in someone's body the divine presence was lost. Mildred and I studied and researched a bit and concluded that this presence was clearly lost in, conservatively estimated, sixteen weeks. By that time bacteria, molds, and tiny insects had reduced the bread to its molecular constituents, and it was no longer "bread." Suddenly, all clothing, purses, and gloves over four months old were de-contaminated! She still wasn't comfortable actually using them, but at least she was able to sell or donate thousands of dollars worth of personal accessories, accumulated over the previous twenty years. It was an economic if not a therapeutic breakthrough.

In my book *Make Someone Happy,* I described a woman who kept her family hungry while she sterilized the kitchen, ostensibly so she wouldn't kill them all with botulism or salmonella. There was pretty clearly a passive-aggressive aspect to her behavior. She was mad at them, for whatever reason, and defended herself against her own angry impulses with a paranoid projection onto the germs and an obsessive-compulsive crusade to eradicate them. She felt herself to be a good mother, while indirectly sticking it to the family she both loved and resented. This kind of passive-aggressiveness is not uncommon as a "secondary gain" in OCD. She could feel noble while starving her family. Nor is this kind of contamination phobia terribly unusual. My son Karl ran across one while working as a grocery store cashier. He had a customer who insisted he scrub down and sterilize the conveyor belt before she would place her food items on it. All her meat products were shrink-wrapped and pre-bagged, yet she insisted they might be contaminated with salmonella. It wasn't at all clear how washing the conveyor would help or why she also insisted a fifty-dollar purchase be divided and charged to two different credit cards. Karl didn't quite recognize this as OCD, but he sure knew it was weird, and he sure knew the woman was controlling and annoying, costing him a good five minutes. I worked with another patient, "Artie O'Dactill," who was a master at this kind of maneuver.

Artie was clever and witty and deep down a very generous fellow, but, sadly, he was also something of a pig. Artie weighed over 400 pounds because he was a compulsive eater. The OCD part was that he ate sweet snacks, always in sets of seven, because he had been sexually abused at that age. Seven muffins, seven cupcakes, seven chocolates, or seven dozen doughnuts, but always seven at a time. He was magically turning seven into something pleasurable instead of painful and perhaps putting up a protective wall of flesh to guard against further abuse. Understandably enough, Artie had a tremendous fear of intimacy and he further protected himself against people getting too close by purposely "pissing people off." If there was a major league for passive-aggressiveness, Artie would have been an All-Star every year. His behavior could be really swinish. For example, since I referred him to an African American psychiatrist for medication, he figured I liked black people and so began telling me racially offensive jokes. Unfortunately, he was quite correct; Dr. Barnett was a close colleague and dear friend. I asked Artie to cease and desist, explaining that I was offended by his slurs and racial epithets, but he just couldn't resist. Yet Artie liked and respected Dr. Barnett himself, just as he liked and respected me. His distancing maneuver worked, as the therapeutic relationship just fizzled out in a puff of black smoke.

Mildred had her own passive-aggressive streak. She hated her mother and the sister who her mother favored. When she was about four or five, Mildred had approached her mother in a circle of women, seeking some attention or nurturing. Instead, she'd been rebuffed with the admonition to "get away from me; you're so ugly and stupid." Mildred never forgot or forgave this narcissistic injury and rejection. Worse yet, she internalized it and accepted it as true. In fact, she wasn't ugly, but she thought she was, and so did nothing to enhance her appearance. She wore no make-up and pulled her hair back in a bun that made her look harsh and forbidding. She wasn't stupid either (she earned a Masters in English and teaching awards), but forty years later she still thought she was. And she despised her mother, devaluing the maternal love-object she despaired of obtaining. So she used her "phobia" as an excuse to force her mother, and her sister, to do all the housework, chauffeur her about, and generally accommodate her bizarre, OCD-driven requirements. I told her if the kitchen cabinets needed to be "de-contaminated" it was *her* job to scrub them. She didn't like it, but she did it, and gradually she decided she could live with slightly less sanitary conditions. While I sympathized with Mildred's animosity towards her cruel mother, I couldn't condone her tactics, especially as they served to perpetuate her OCD. I also told her to take on some sort of volunteer work with people less fortunate than herself, in order to focus her interests outward instead of on herself. As Alfred Adler pointed out, neurotics, including obsessive-compulsives, are too self-absorbed and lack sufficient "social interest." It is helpful for them to become more involved with others and to become more concerned with the welfare of persons besides themselves. Her work with the poor gave Mildred a better perspective on life and herself, and many of her rituals simply could not be accommodated in a soup kitchen and had to be abandoned.

When I left Illinois and graduate school to take a position in Austin, I turned Mildred over to another graduate student to continue her treatment. I had gotten her back in church and attending teachers' meetings, and he got her back to Mass and even Communion. Mildred asked to give me a "bonus" check, personally, to help defray my moving expenses. I could not ethically accept her gift, but I was deeply moved by her offer and her faith in and affection for me. She was after all a good and loving person, despite her emotional disturbance.

Obsessive-compulsives come in a number of varieties, and I guess I've probably seen most of them. There are counters, who feel compelled to count light poles or cars or times they chew their food. There are checkers, who must check all the doors and windows twelve times, to be sure they are locked, every time they leave the house, even if they *never* unlock them. There are touchers, who cannot resist the compulsion to touch or stroke certain objects in a ritualistic fashion. I treated a fifteen-year-old who'd been washing the skin off his hands to get rid of germs and perhaps the impulse to masturbate. I've also seen a thirteen-year-old who's afraid Heaven will be boring and feels terribly guilty at her doubt in God's ability to entertain her for all Eternity. She comes from an extremely religious family but also one troubled by severe marital conflict, which undoubtedly was the original source of her anxious thoughts. I taught her that she was misunderstanding the meaning of the word "eternal." It doesn't mean lasting forever, but rather "existing outside of time." That is, eternity lasts a single infinitely glorious moment. Did she believe God could do that? She did, and her fears were much alleviated by this thought. Another patient counted her footsteps or recited silly doggerel (about her dog!) in order to distract her from intrusive and unpleasant thoughts. It worked so well she no longer remembered what the thoughts were, but she couldn't stop for fear they'd return. I saw a kid who had to brush off a chair before he sat down and after he stood up and had to sweep a doorway with his hands before walking through it. He could not say why, but it made him terribly anxious not to do it. With him I used two standard OCD behavioral treatments, "Response Prevention" and "Response Cost." With the first technique, the patient is instructed not to allow himself to act out the ritual. His anxiety will rise tremendously, but if he persists, the anxiety will gradually fade away over time, and the compulsive ritual will slowly be extinguished. With the second technique, the patient is allowed to act out the compulsive ritual, but must do it at some cost, thereby discouraging him from repeating it. With this boy, I told him either to refrain from his brushing and sweeping or to do it fifty times on each occasion. It sounds a little cruel, but it did help. Often medicine can help too, sometimes dramatically wiping out OCD symptoms almost immediately. This is one reason many psychologists believe OCD has a strong biological basis, at least in some cases. In any case, people with obsessive-compulsive disorder are truly suffering and have a real battle on their hands. I have to admire their courage and tenacity, even if I can't buy their logic.

CHAPTER FIVE

"'Til Death..."

OVER THE COURSE OF MY career as a psychologist, I've dealt with hundreds of suicidal patients, including dozens of people who tried it and failed. At some point, often immediately, every one of them was glad it hadn't worked and they were still alive. I happened to be in her hospital room when one of my patients awoke from a suicidal overdose. Her first words were, "God, I'm glad I'm still alive." Another patient shot off half his face, then, instead of finishing the job, crawled a half mile through the woods to safety. Several corrective surgeries later, he was a happy guy who was glad to be alive and who no longer allowed himself to be stressed out by his work or family problems. He even calmly handled his *daughter's* attempted suicide. The daughter also decided to live, perhaps partly due to a cute new boyfriend. Any reason is a good one. It's worth thinking about if you're ever contemplating your own demise.

Unfortunately, a lot of suicides do surprisingly little contemplating before committing this ultimate act of desperation. Suicidal people lack perspective, electing to use a permanent solution for what is usually a temporary problem. Many suicide attempts are essentially impulsive responses to a momentary situation, done with little or no thought and sometimes for the silliest of reasons. My first suicide case was like this, in fact even humorously so.

While still in graduate school, I was doing a clinical practicum at the University of Illinois Counseling Center. Most of my patients were undergraduates who were homesick and depressed, confused about selecting a major, smoking too much pot, or otherwise stressed out by college life and the world away from home. Also a few faculty wives talking about extramarital affairs, either their own or their husbands'. One patient was a young girl who'd consulted me a few times about her career choices, dealing with her parents, and similar issues. She called me one night, asking to meet me on an emergency basis, as she was seriously thinking of killing herself. We met at the Student Center and she told me her story:

She was romantically involved with a young man of whom her parents disapproved. As it was nearing the end of the spring semester, the two would be parting, each returning to their parents' homes for the summer. They lived in different towns, and her parents would not allow her to visit. Thus, they'd be separated for three months.

"If I can't see my boyfriend for the whole summer," she declared, "I'd rather die. That's why I'm going to kill myself." I said what any reasonable person with a little perspective would, which is about 90 percent of what you do in therapy.

"If you kill yourself," I pointed out, "you won't see him in the fall, either."

She was stunned. "Oh," she said. "I hadn't thought of that. Gosh, I'm sorry I bothered you."

The threat of suicide vanished, leaving an embarrassed but still vibrant young lady. A therapeutic triumph, and it only took one sentence. Actually, we talked about how to approach her parents, and she was able to negotiate a compromise and see her boyfriend at home. Besides being misguided and short-sighted, her suicide wasn't necessary, being based on erroneous information.

They haven't all been that easy, though the odds are usually in favor of the therapist's succeeding. If someone wants to talk to you about suicide there must be at least some part of him that wants you to talk him out of it. The ones who are really determined to die don't call, even to say good-bye. They just go off and do it. The only one I've ever lost was a charming but confused young woman who'd stopped seeing me six months earlier, as she was doing fine. She didn't call me or anyone else, and she left no note. She just jumped off a building, leaving me and her family and friends to wonder why. It's a pretty sad legacy.

I guess you could also count another patient who'd also quit therapy and more-or-less committed suicide. He was a hot-tempered and very impulsive college athlete who shot himself playing "Russian Roulette," a game that must be considered self-destructive if not frankly suicidal.

People kill themselves for all sorts of reasons, some seemingly trivial, even comical, some considerably more serious. I've seen suicide attempts in reaction to a bad grade, a lost job, the death of a pet, the diagnosis of a terminal illness. In my experience the most common trigger for suicide is the break-up of a love affair. When I was running the Adolescent Unit at Hill Crest, we admitted a sixteen-year-old boy who'd put a rifle bullet through his chest just a few days earlier. Remarkably, he'd hit no major organs, bones, or blood vessels, and he was medically fine. He'd shot himself while talking on the phone to his girlfriend. She was dumping him, and he was trying either to talk her into staying with him or make her feel bad for rejecting him. Either way, it evidently didn't work. Meanwhile, it took about three days of psychotherapy for him to decide the girl was a "bitch" and he didn't like her anyway. He just couldn't handle being the dumpee instead of the dumper. Three years later he called me looking for a letter of reference to one of the military academies. I wrote him a good one, figuring a guy who could shoot with this precision would be a real asset to our Armed Forces.

Of course, the break-up of a relationship, while certainly painful, is a poor reason for committing suicide. Suicide won't save the relationship, and it effectively prevents you from finding another one. There are nearly eight billion people out there, and half of them are the right gender for you. That's pretty good odds, even considering that half of those are Indians and Chinese you're not likely ever to meet. Everybody needs somebody some time, but it is a mistake to center all your happiness, indeed your very life, on one particular somebody. Life is too tenuous. It's your job to make yourself happy in life, and you can do so without any particular other person, difficult though that may be. People survive and go on to find meaning and happiness even after losing their life's partner. Besides, the level of dependency suggested by a suicide following a break-up does not speak well for the quality of that relationship. A good relationship should help you to be happier and more independent, not less so.

Oftentimes the suicide attempt, or threat thereof, is part of an extortion racket: "If you leave me, I'll kill myself." Amazingly, this often works quite well. I saw one beautiful, sweet young woman who stayed on a couple of years with an absolute jerk, because he used this threat whenever she tried to leave him. He drank too much and worked too little, was living largely off her money, and was at least verbally abusive. She no longer loved or even liked him, but she felt responsible for him and felt she couldn't handle the guilt if he suicided. It took a while, but I finally convinced her that he was a controlling, manipulative bum who was only using her and probably making idle threats. She came to realize that no person can be made responsible for another person's life. If you want to kill yourself, that's your business, even if you want to suicide over me. She finally dumped him and got on with her life. He immediately found a new sucker and moved in with her without even the slightest hint of suicide. She took a risk, but in my estimation, it wasn't a very big one. Guys like that are generally too selfish and too chicken to sacrifice themselves over another person.

Some suicide attempts are so melodramatic they are obviously ploys for attention. One patient's family called around midnight, saying she'd disappeared, leaving a suicide note. From our discussions I knew where she'd be and sent them to the cemetery in which her father was buried. There was her car, a garden hose running from the tailpipe to where she sat inside. Fortunately for her, the hot exhaust had melted the cheap plastic hose and was monoxodizing only the surrounding gravestones. A few days in the psych unit and she was fine, except for a bad headache and a sense of embarrassment.

Suicidal threats are not to be taken lightly, however. It is a myth that people who talk about suicide, or threaten to kill themselves, are just bluffing and won't do it. Actually, research indicates that most suicides at least hinted at it before acting. That doesn't mean everybody who says, "I wish I were dead" needs to be locked up in a hospital. It does mean that someone needs to listen and see if that person needs help. As in other areas of psychology (and life), the rule is to "react, but don't overreact." A lot of suicidal talk is just talk, and a lot of attempts are really just "gestures," but a lot aren't. It often takes a trained professional to tell the difference, and we're far from infallible ourselves. When in doubt, however, get a consult, even if it makes the person angry. Better mad than dead.

Many suicides are calculated to hurt somebody else, usually in revenge for having been hurt. You broke up with me but I'm going to kill myself and make you feel guilty. "You'll be sad when I'm gone, you rascal you." I see this a lot in young people, who often have a naive and unrealistic view of life and love anyway. I think of it as the "Tom Sawyer Fantasy." Remember how Tom and Huck got stranded downriver and were given up for dead? They finally straggled back to town several days later, just in time to hide in the choir loft and witness their own funeral service. It did their little hearts (and big egos) good to hear the sweet words of praise and wails of lament voiced by the preacher and congregation. Tom's Aunt Polly even cried for Huck, declaring that he wasn't really such a bad boy, just misunderstood. There's nothing like death to make a saint out of a sinner. Many young people have shared with me the fantasy of hearing their loved ones mourn their loss. They believe they will derive satisfaction from the guilt and remorse of those who have slighted, mistreated, or rejected them. What they fail to consider is that if you kill yourself, you won't be in the balcony listening to the beautiful eulogies. You'll be the guy in the box.

And that's what I point out to these would-be suicidal teenagers, sometimes describing in fairly graphic detail what really happens to you after you die: what the embalmer does to you, the process of decay, and how much you'll hurt the people you leave behind. Breaking up the fantasy makes some of them pretty angry but also a lot less inclined to suicide.

If this sounds a bit hostile on my part, it probably is. I've just seen too many family members and friends who've been devastated by a suicide. It's an injury that is not soon healed. Further, my attitude mirrors that of the suicide herself. We tend to think of suicide as an act of depression and desperation, and most times it is. But it is also an act of hostility and aggression. It is in fact an act of murder, even if the life you take happens to be your own. Moreover, it's often done to hurt others, the ultimate in passive-aggressiveness. That's pretty hostile, and it's why survivors of suicide are angry as well as sad. Indeed, their anger and "survivor guilt" further complicate and delay their process of mourning. What a gift to leave your loved ones.

The hostility inherent in suicide is even more dramatically evident in suicide/homicides—that is, in cases where someone murders his family and then kills himself. The only active patient I've lost was a victim of such a crime. She was a frazzled-looking banker of about forty, who came in with her lover, a nice but nondescript guy about the same age. She was leaving her husband to be with the lover and wanted to leave the husband with me for safekeeping. He was an extremely dependent and abusive alcoholic who had threatened to kill her and himself if she ever left him. I agreed to see him the next day and cautioned her not to go home or to communicate with him in any way, beyond telling him the appointment time. Even though most such threats are manipulative bluffs, some are not, and it wasn't worth risking it with this one. "React, but don't overreact." She didn't go home, but she did go to the bank, and he shot her dead in the parking deck. The police found his body a few days later.

Incidentally, this case took on a note of macabre humor for me and my staff. After hearing the television account of the murder, my secretary ran upstairs to borrow the landlord's newspaper for more details. We were shocked and horrified at the event, yet perversely thrilled by our close encounter with this tragic, sensational murder. Then the husband called our office to verify his appointment time! Now we were scared. Was he coming to shoot me too, perhaps seeing me a co-conspirator in his wife's perfidious betrayal? We called the police and shut the office down for the rest of the day. It turned out to be the landlord calling, pretending to be the husband. He was a good friend but an unfunny jokester, and we cussed him out pretty thoroughly for his prank. The police detective also failed to see the humor in this impersonation, and I believe they also had a little chat.

I've seen all kinds of people make all kinds of suicide attempts, overdosing on everything from aspirin to iodine to cleaning solvents. I had a patient ("Dorothy," described in Chapter 13 on multiple personality disorder) who told me every week for two years that she was "more suicidal than ever right now." This woman routinely cut herself with a knife and kept a noose hanging in her attic, for whenever she might need it. In fact, knowing she could cash in her chips at any time was all that gave her the courage to stay in the game at all. I've seen several people who shot themselves and survived, including one poor lady who ballistically amputated the tip of her ear and a man who put a sizable new dimple in one cheek. But my most bizarre suicide attempt was one that happened right before my eyes.

"Lara" was another multiple personality case I was willing to see only in the hospital, because she was too volatile to see as an outpatient. A large but pretty woman in her thirties, Lara had as a child been repeatedly brutalized by her father, a missionary to South America. The memories of these awful events were encapsulated in her various "alter" personalities, and thus were not consciously available to the "Lara" persona. In our sessions Lara would frequently "switch" to one of these alters who would then flash back to an abuse episode, re-experiencing it as if it was actually happening again. I would try to help her remember and reprocess these events, in order to re-integrate her split and shattered consciousness.

The suicide attempt occurred in Lara's hospital room, as she sat on her bed and I sat in a chair beside her. As usual, she went into a flashback, this time of her father sodomizing her with an ice pick. (For those skeptical of such abuse or of MPD in general, there was solid medical evidence for this rape.) Acting out this memory, Lara rolled over and pulled a sheet over her, writhing about, screaming, and repeatedly crying, "No, Daddy, it hurts; it hurts." Awful as it is to witness such a re-enactment, I was getting used to it and was aware there was nothing I could do to stop it. Even ice water in her face had failed before to end a flashback. I just had to wait for it to run its course. Finally, Lara stopped crying and was still. In fact, she was too still. Recalling an earlier session in which Lara had tried to choke herself (she was very strong and was trained as a nurse; she knew just where to put her hands, and I'd had to work hard to wrestle them away from her throat), I called to her softly to wake up. She didn't answer. "Lara." Again, no answer. Becoming concerned, I tugged at the sheet which she'd tucked tightly around her. Finally getting it off her, I was aghast to see that Lara's face was blue. Wrapped tightly around her neck, twisted and held there by her hands, with her whole body (250 pounds plus) holding it in position, was the strangest suicide weapon I've ever seen—a pastel pink baby blanket. I hollered "Code Blue" and began trying to disentangle the blanket, not an easy task considering Lara's weight. This being a psychiatric hospital, the nurses were a bit uncertain how we could have a Code Blue ("patient not breathing"), and by the time they came running to help I had the blanket off and Lara breathing again. It gives a whole new meaning to the concept of "suicide precautions" when a patient nearly dies on a locked ward, her doctor in attendance, using a baby blanket. And try explaining this event to a jury in a malpractice suit.

I know of an equally bizarre hospital suicide, this one successful. On a locked unit in the same hospital, on maximum suicide precautions, a patient took his life by crushing his skull with his hospital bed. He put his head between the raisable foot of the bed and the bed's metal frame, then lowered the bed using a remote control.

Ultimately there is very little humor in suicide, however you choose to do it. If I've ever prevented a single death, and I believe I have, then my career has been gratifying. Lara, unfortunately, didn't make it. We transferred her to the state hospital where she quickly conned her way out. She successfully asphyxiated herself two weeks later.

I should mention in passing a last variant on suicide, which might be called "passive suicide" or "suicide by proxy." It is well known that some people commit suicide by committing a crime and confronting the police in such a way that they are compelled to shoot them. "Suicide by cop," it's called. My variant was similar, consisting of a devout Christian who wanted to die but believed it a grievous sin to take her own life. When I first saw her she'd been driving around for five days and nights, with no sleep, no food, and no water, hoping she'd have a wreck and be killed. Blessed, or lucky, she ended up being one of my favorite and most memorable patients instead. ("Barbara," also described in the second MPD chapter.)

If this book should ever fall into the hands of a would-be suicide, I hope these stories will convince him not to. I hope he'll get into treatment instead. There may be cases in which suicide is the best course of action for all concerned, but in all my years of practice. I haven't seen any yet. I can honestly say that I've never seriously considered suicide, and I do not consider it "normal" to do so. I can certainly envision circumstances in which I would consider it a viable option—terminal cancer, for example. But for more solvable problems in living, no. Homicide, maybe, but not the Big S. Find another answer. Let someone help you. I've seen too many former suicide patients go on to live happy, productive lives for you not to be one of them.

CHAPTER SIX

Dramatic Breakthroughs and One-Shot Wonders

TO MY RECOLLECTION THERE HAVE been only two successful TV series featuring psychotherapists, *The Bob Newhart Show* and *Frasier*. Both were comedies, not dramas, and both focused largely on their character's *non*-professional life. That's because psychotherapy is mostly not very dramatic and often tedious, if not boring. It is complicated and sequential, so it's difficult to portray a patient's progress without showing the entire course of therapy, extending perhaps to many years. It involves ideas and emotions and memories, all of which are difficult to present visually. Most people find psychiatry and psychology interesting but the therapy itself pretty dull. The few dramatic breakthroughs that do occur are mental events meaningful mainly to the doctor and patient alone. So we focus our TV sets on Newhart's colleagues and office staff and a few eccentric patients, or on Frasier's funny but dysfunctional family, more than on the therapy itself. If this book ever makes the big screen, I doubt they'll get Brad Pitt to play me.

But now and again therapy does get dramatic, especially where a major breakthrough or even a "cure" occurs in one fateful session. Here are a few from my own experience.

The scariest session I ever had (apart from the ones described above with "Lara") followed a phone call from the Eastside Mental Health

Center, where I still worked part-time. One of my patients had shown up with a gun and was demanding to see me immediately. I was busy at my private practice, and I'm ordinarily prone to decline invitations delivered at gunpoint, but the police and the Center Director were pretty insistent on my attending their little party. I reluctantly rescheduled my next two appointments and headed anxiously towards my rendezvous with the potential Shootist. The SWAT team escorted me through their lines and ushered me into the day treatment center where "John" was holed up with my old buddy and colleague Gary Stockdale. John greeted me with a slight smile, which gave me a little reassurance about my safety. Still, the action end of that rifle looked awfully big, and I wasn't at all sure of John's intentions. Gary looked concerned but not really nervous, and he'd done a good job keeping John calm and communicating. John was pacing back and forth, rifle in hand, ranting about his desire to shoot somebody and displaying two pockets full of bullets, lest anyone doubt the lethality of his threat. I tried to remember if Sigmund Freud had anything helpful to say about this kind of situation, but nothing came to mind. Did the great Doctor ever have days like this?

When I asked John what was up he told me he'd been laid off from his factory job for fighting with a co-worker. He'd pulled a knife on the man, an offense resulting in automatic dismissal. Still, he was angry at the boss and felt he'd been treated unfairly. As it turned out, this was not his first on-the-job fight and not his first lay-off. Truth was, his wife had had it with his impulsive violence and frequent lay-offs or walk-offs. She was ready to walk out herself, and John was feeling pretty scared and desperate. He was ready to take someone down with him if that's where he was headed. He'd also boxed himself into a real corner with no clear avenue of escape and no way to save face and keep from looking like a fool. The cops were ready for action, the wife needed more than an apology; and he'd look pretty silly if no shots were fired. John had impulsively escalated a bad situation into a potentially disastrous one. Gary looked at me like a quarterback who'd just handed off the ball in the face of a total blitz. I felt like a high-school halfback facing the Dallas Cowboy defense.

Fortunately, the situation was momentarily stable, thanks mostly to Gary, and John had no real plan. He didn't even have a real target. He just wanted somebody to bail him out and he was ready for suggestions. So I just kept him talking while I tried to think of some kind of strategy. Then I made what turned out to be a crucial intervention. I sat down. We'd been standing and talking for over an hour, near the end of a hectic and now frightening day, and I was tired. I said as much to John and asked if he didn't mind me having a seat. He was okay with that, so I eased on into a chair and propped my feet on another. Gary did the same. John kept pacing back and forth carrying his rifle, but he'd been on his feet longer than I had, and he was even more scared than I was. He seemed to be casting envious glances at Gary and me, who were now quite comfortable.

"That rifle's got to be getting pretty heavy, John," I suggested. "Why don't you take a load off (pun intended) and have a seat? Here, set the gun on the table where you can still reach it quicker than I can." John gratefully sank into a chair and gingerly put the gun on the table in front of him. The tension eased palpably.

Sitting down changed the whole situation. You don't sit with your feet up and threaten to kill somebody. It's just not proper. We were collaborators now, not adversaries. We were on the same side, looking for a mutual solution. John was looking tired and a bit sheepish by now. He really didn't want to hurt anybody, he explained. He just wanted his job back so his wife wouldn't kill him.

"Look," I said, "I've been treating you for depression, right? Dr. Morrison's got you on some medicine, right? What if I called your boss and explained how depression can make people a little nuts, reassured him you'll be okay and got you a couple days off instead of being fired? Would that convince you to put the gun up and go home quietly?"

"Sure as hell would," John replied.

I'd been relying pretty much on gut instinct so far. Sitting down, for example, felt like a good move, but I was not really consciously aware of why this tactic was helpful. But now I knew in a rational way that I was on the right track to resolve this matter. There remained only the minor issues of the boss and the gun, the wife and the cops.

"Okay, let's go make the call. There's a phone in my office we can use." And then I took a small risk. "You can't take the gun in there. Leave it here with Gary. He's been around guns all his life (a lie), and he'll know how to take care of it safely." John handed over the rifle and we headed for the phone. It was over.

John's boss bought the explanation and let him return to work after a brief medical leave. A few weeks later he got into another scuffle and was again handed his pink slip, this time without further uproar. The cops let John off with a warning, though they confiscated the gun. Gary was hardly the gun expert I'd portrayed him as being, but he was able to determine that the rifle was not actually loaded, which is why the police were so forgiving. Still, John was carrying enough ammunition to back up his bluff if necessary. I'm glad I decided to "sit" on the matter instead of challenging him or forcing his hand.

There's a whole school of family therapy centering on the notion that one strategic intervention can dramatically change family or lead to a patient's recovery. It's surprising how often a single comment can throw a whole new light on the therapy. "Reframing" is a good example of this technique. In reframing one simply relabels the patient's behavior or problem, changing its complexion by giving it a different name, one which the patient is competent to deal with. The results can be dramatic. For example, I saw a seventeen-year-old who was so depressed he could not study at all. He was in danger of imminent failure (from advanced classes), and his parents were very concerned. He himself asked for my help. He wanted to learn how to motivate and discipline himself. I agreed to try my best and, just to be safe, I asked his dad if he wanted his son to follow my program. He did, and he told his son to follow my advice to the letter. It was an important request.

I suggested the boy—we'll call him "Junior"—spend only five minutes studying that night, then reward himself with a video game and a small bag of chips. After all, he'd not studied at all for weeks. Five minutes was real progress. Tomorrow night he should do ten minutes only, again followed by a reward. Add five minutes each night until he was up to an hour or so, and always working towards a self-imposed goal and self-rewarded treat. Standard behavior modification. I also told Junior to keep a nightly log, recording how much time he's studied, whether he'd met his goal or not. He agreed, and Dad told him this was *his* direction as well.

Next week Junior and parents returned as instructed. But Junior, depressed as he was, had not studied at all. Zero, Zip, Nada. Mom and Dad were very worried and a little perturbed, but they didn't know how to deal with a depressed adolescent. Should they apply more pressure and risk worsening his depression, or back off and risk academic failure? Not an easy choice. I asked to see Junior's log book, but he had nothing to show. "I didn't keep a record because I didn't study any," he explained. But I had instructed him to keep a log whether he met his study goal or not. I turned to his father and asked what it was called when you told your kid to do something and he didn't do it. "Disobedience," he replied. I asked if he knew how to handle a disobedient child. "Sure enough do," he grinned, and turned to Junior with newfound authority.

"Son, you have disobeyed me by not following this doctor's program. You will be studying an hour tonight and every night from now on or there'll be hell to pay. You got me?"

I'd redefined the problem from one of depression, which Junior's parents did not know how to treat, to one of disobedience, which was well within their area of expertise. Dad took charge and acted with wisdom and authority.

Junior's hand had been called, but he didn't fold easily. "I won't do it," he declared, "and if you try to make me, I'll run away from home."

"Son," answered his dad, "you do what you gotta do, and I'll do what I gotta. The rule stands." I sent them home and waited for results.

The dad called later that evening. Junior had run off, just like he threatened to, so what was our next move? I asked if Junior had run away before. He had. On each occasion he'd waited a few hours, called home, and returned, with no consequences and no rules enforced. "You've got him," I said, "but you've got to take a chance." "Deal me in," said Dad. I told him when Junior called to say he would come home, he should be informed that he was welcome only if he'd abide by the house rules. That meant an hour's study every night. Sure enough, Junior called, and Dad called his bluff. "An hour a night." Junior allowed as how he'd be home in twenty minutes, and he was.

When I saw Junior a week later he was studying two hours a night and was happy as a card sharp with a newly marked deck. His depression had miraculously disappeared. Once I'd put the problem into his area of competence, Dad had handled it quite effectively. Dad and Mom and I then worked briefly on a marital problem, which may have been the source of Junior's depression in the first place.

It's amazing how capable families can be if you simply redefine a problem in terms they can understand. "Depression" is medical and mysterious, but "disobedience" is easily handled with a little discipline. Interestingly, this relabeling can work in the opposite direction as well. When parents understand that their child is truly suffering from a disease (depression) they will allow him to get some help and quit being so punitive, which will often give the "bad" child new hope and new motivation to succeed.

Good therapy is good therapy, no matter what theoretical approach underlies it. Therapists from very different schools will come up with the same intervention, even though they explain it quite differently. Thus, my friend Dr. Paul Weir and I can usually agree on what a case is all about and how to treat it, even though his training is psychoanalytic and my own is behavioral and family systems. One of my favorite one-shot "cures" illustrated the point so well that I published a case study on it in *Family Systems Medicine*. (Also reprinted in Italian as a chapter in *Famiglia E Malattia Psicosomatica*, edited by Luigi Onnis.) It was a true one-shot wonder and made sense in terms of family systems theory as well as behavior modification. I didn't work up the Freudian viewpoint, but I suspect Paul could crank it out convincingly enough. Something about Oedipus, no doubt.

"Peter" was a moderately obese ten-year-old, referred by a pediatrician who recognized that his problems were not limited to enuresis and encopresis (wetting the bed and soiling his pants). Peter was only five when his father committed suicide, and he reacted by wetting the bed every night and soiling his pants at least twice daily ever since. Peter was pudgy, clumsy, fearful, and highly dependent on his mother, with whom he still slept. That's right, he was wetting *her* bed. He alternately clung to her dependently and defied her angrily. These behaviors did nothing to ingratiate him to his peers, who rejected him for a total "nerd." He had no siblings and no friends, did poorly in school, and had no identifiable self-esteem. What could he possibly feel good about?

Peter's mother was also somewhat over-weight and was as dependent on him as he was on her. Feeling chronically depressed and guilty—Peter's father had killed himself because she'd divorced him over his drinking—her only companions were Peter and her own mother. Grandmother babied Peter terribly, under-cutting mother's authority and keeping her in a subservient position. Peter was undisciplined, manipulative, and whiney. He also smelled bad.

In family therapy terms, Peter and his mother were "enmeshed," and the generational boundaries between grandmother, mother, and child were vague and inappropriate. Mother was powerless and considered incompetent, which her son's problems constantly reconfirmed. Grandmother, who'd disliked Peter's father and repeatedly run him off, also felt guilty, and pampered Peter to make up for his father's loss. Mother had never really been able to grow up and leave her own mother, which had led to more husbandly drinking and the failure of the marriage. She resented her mother, yet was dependent on her emotionally and financially. Peter was in a kind of inappropriate coalition with his grandmother and therefore out of Mother's control. Ridiculed by his peers, he ran home where he was spoiled and allowed to act like a baby.

In behavioral terms, Peter was oppositional and regressive. His discipline was highly inconsistent and his misbehavior was actually being rewarded by gaining him excessive nurturance and control over his family. He needed clear expectations and clear consequences for both good and bad behaviors, and he was receiving neither. Fortunately his mother "Rita" was getting pretty sick of the whole mess and was ready to kick some "booty." Five years in a wet bed, stinky underwear, and being disenfranchised in her own home had finally gotten to her.

I ended our first meeting by instructing Rita in how to regain control over Peter and over her own life. She was to put him in his own bed and insist he sleep there, beginning that same night, and enforcing it with a spanking if necessary. She was to establish a system of rewards for "dry nights" and "clean days" and have Peter do his own laundry and bed-making when he had an "accident." She was to inform her mother that discipline was *her* job, and Grandmother was not to interfere. Finally, she was to begin going out alone or with other adults and leave Peter to find his own playmates. One mutual activity was encouraged: join Weight Watchers.

Rita understood the rationale for this plan and gladly agreed to it. Peter was afraid and didn't like it all, and he began begging and cajoling and demanding to sleep with Mom before he even left my office. He kept it up for the next six hours, with Rita firmly responding, "No." When Grandmother predictably intervened on Peter's behalf, Rita turned to her and said, "I'm gonna tell you like the psychologist told me—butt out!" Grandmother was appalled, but she retreated from the fray and soon began to back up Rita's discipline. Finally, at two in the morning, Peter stumbled wearily but doggedly into his mother's bedroom, complaining that he could not sleep in his own bed because his father's ghost was haunting him! It was a great line and a psychologically accurate metaphor for the family's pathology; they were indeed haunted by the memory of Dad's suicide.

Rita later reported, "My heart stopped, but I remembered what you said. So I grabbed a switch, looked him cold in the eye, and said, 'bullshit.'" Peter slept peacefully, if tearfully, in his own bed, and he continued to do so for at least the four months I followed him. And in the morning his sheets were dry.

The effects on Peter of this intervention were most salutary. From that first session on he became more independent, more obedient, and more pleasant. He astonished his mom the day after by announcing first that he was going out to play with his friends (if he had permission) and second that he needed to replace his nerdy leather shoes with some new Nikes. He returned several hours later with a recently bloodied nose and a huge grin. His outer garments were filthy, but his underwear was clean.

I saw Peter and Rita about a month later and followed up in three more months with a phone call. I made no other therapeutic interventions. By the end of four months Peter's bed-wetting was down to less than one night a week, and his encopresis had ceased abruptly and entirely. He'd lost nine and a half pounds, and Rita had lost fifteen. He'd made some new friends and was now known as "Pete." Rita wasn't dating yet ("ten more pounds") but was looking for an apartment for Peter and herself, while remaining on good terms with her mother.

When folks are ready to make a move, all you have to do is point the right direction and stand back. Peter and Rita were primed and ready to fire, and every theory I knew showed me the target's direction. I wished it was always so easy, except a two-session treatment wasn't much good for my business.

Enuresis is primarily a sleep disorder, the result of sleeping too soundly. It is often seen in children with ADHD, who are also prone to sleep-walking and -talking, and, occasionally, to very intense and realistic "hypnogogic hallucinations" or nightmares. It is less commonly a problem of internal plumbing, requiring medical attention. It is infrequently an indication of an emotional disorder, mostly because anxiety and depression interfere with proper sleep. But enuresis is rarely an act of defiance. Even the dullest child can conjure up a way to rebel that does not entail looking like a baby and lying in his own pee. Encopresis, on the other hand, is often an act of rebellion, a graphic, if passive-aggressive, way of saying, "shit on you."

Take "Funky Freddie" for example. Sly and devious beyond his first-grade years, Freddie had perfected the coprophilic art of encopresis on demand. His teacher was cute, nice, and talented, but to Freddie she was a villain and an adversary. If she dared to scold or correct him, Freddie would walk slowly to her desk, smile crookedly and let loose with a mini but stinky bowel movement. Then he'd sit in splendid isolation as the fumes rose around him and classmates fled in disgust.

Encopresis can also be used more subtly, as a power tactic in a parent-child battle. Here, too, the right intervention at the right time can turn things around very quickly. A mother I'll call "Delilah" consulted me about her nearly four-year-old son named "Samson." Despite Delilah's best efforts, the young Prince was completely un-potty-trained. He tried peeing in the pot once, then announced he didn't like it and would not replicate this accomplishment. He wouldn't even try sitting on it, not even on the warm plastic baby seat. The diaper was just fine by him, thank you very much, and you could forget that other stuff. Delilah tried rewarding good performances with ice cream and Disney videos. "Thanks, but no thanks," said Samson. She tried punishing him with time-out and with cleaning up his own pants. "Not a problem," said the strong-man. "I'll pull the house down before I go doo-doo in the pot." Delilah put mineral oil in his food, but he still wouldn't "go" until she put a diaper on him. Then he'd head for the nearest corner, squat, and ask to be changed. Delilah refused to change Samson's diaper. Fine, he'd live happily with a poop-filled pantie, even though his bottom got red and raw.

A parent has to pick his or her battles carefully. Kids will get you into a power struggle, and it's essential that you win. But sometimes you just can't. Samson and Delilah were locked into a fierce power struggle, but he held a distinct home-court advantage. It was, after all, *his* bowels they were contending over. She'd tried begging, enticing, cajoling, persuading, demanding, rewarding, punishing, and praying, and all he'd done was—nothing. Game, set, and match, Samson.

I praised Delilah for her efforts and her concern. I pointed out she'd tried every reasonable, rational approach and asked if she was ready now to try something crazy. She was, though not at first. I told her to quit trying to make Samson use the toilet and start pushing

Pampers. Take him to the K-Mart and buy a case of diapers. Let him hear you bragging to your girlfriends what a wonderful, sweet child you have, who uses a nice, neat diaper instead of making you clean a dirty old potty seat. Don't let him near the pot and push Pampers instead. "That's crazy," said Delilah, but she agreed to try anyway.

She called me a couple of days later. Sammy was refusing to wear a diaper. He was insisting on using the toilet, for both number one and number two. Delilah didn't quite know what to do. "Keep trying to push the diapers," I told her. "Then give in grudgingly. Let him 'win' and use the toilet." It was simple "reverse psychology" but it worked. Lucky my adversary was a toddler.

What's interesting is that Delilah told me she had another family problem. Her husband was trying to force her to have anal sex with him, a practice she found utterly disgusting. The poor lady was caught in two power struggles, one for control of her baby's butt, the other for control of her own. How meaningful was the parallel? I'll never know for sure, but family therapists do describe "isomorphic" transactions in family systems. These are actions or relations in different areas, but taking the same form. Anorexics, for example, may be saying behaviorally that they are "fed up" with parental conflict and "can't stomach" any more control by them.

The paradoxical or reverse psychology approach isn't guaranteed every time, but it works often enough to be extremely useful. It cuts neatly through parent-child power struggles and enables stubborn kids to change without them or their parents losing face. It does require a certain degree of acting ability on the parents' part, however. Here's part of a letter from the mother of another poopy-pants toddler, to illustrate the point:

"Chase's pediatric gastroenterologist vetoed your daily suppository idea, and our initial attempts at reverse psychology failed: He was happy to put on a diaper when we suggested it. However, an offhand comment his Dad made to Chase on our daughter's first birthday finally did the trick. He said Darlene was growing up too fast and we really liked babies, so would Chase mind just staying our baby? He could keep pooping in his pants, sleep in the crib, use his pacifier again, etc. Chase was visibly horrified and said no, he was a big boy, and Dad said that was fine, but if he decided he wanted to stay our baby, that would be great.

"Later that night, Chase began to go in his underwear, and his Dad started clapping and cheering, calling for me and saying Chase had decided to stay our baby. Chase got up and RAN for the potty, telling me to get his underwear down quick, before he went in his pants. He had one accident the next day, but after that, he's done it in the potty every time . . . Thank you for your help in this extraordinarily difficult time."

And give Dad the Golden Diaper Award for best actor in a potty drama.

More than anything else, what a therapist offers a patient is a good, common-sense perspective on the problem. Most one-shot therapeutic successes result from a clear statement of what ought to be obvious, then working through whatever is keeping the patient from doing it. For example, a middle-aged woman with epilepsy complained to me that her children and grandchildren spent very little time with her. Because of her illness she could not drive, and with Birmingham's inadequate bus system and rare and expensive taxis, she was completely dependent on friends and family for her transportation. Their avoidance of her was a real problem, as well as hurting her feelings. On and on she moaned and whined and complained about how rough her life was. She never got to go anywhere; she was lonely; her meager and fixed income was wasted on filthy cabs. Her medicine made her drowsy, and her back hurt, and she was afraid of the people on the bus. She griped and carried on for forty-five minutes before I finally stopped her.

"Mrs. Ratchet, do you talk to your family and friends the way you are talking to me?" She guessed that she did. "Well, maybe that's why they don't want to spend time with you," I suggested. "Forgive me for being blunt, but I'm having a hard time listening to you, and I'm getting *paid* for it. I can imagine how your family must feel."

She was shocked and probably a bit offended, though I'd tried to be as nice as I could about telling her the unpleasant truth.

After a minute she said, "Thank you. You're undoubtedly correct, and I needed to hear that, difficult as it is. I think I'll change how I talk to my family." Which she did, with obvious salutary results. She even made some new friends with the other bus riders.

Sometimes you don't even need to state the truth; it speaks for itself. A seventeen-year-old was brought to see me because he'd been caught smoking dope. He was unconcerned and not interested in my sermon-ette on the evils of drug abuse. He saw no reason to quit. "What's the harm?" he asked. "My grades are fine; the health risks are essentially nonexistent; and nobody gets busted anymore." The kid was basically right. U.S. laws on substance use make very little sense. One drug kills more people than all other drugs combined—tobacco. The real killer drug is nicotine, followed distantly by alcohol, both of which are legal. Marijuana is fairly harmless and even has proven medicinal value, yet it is against the law in many states. It doesn't make sense, and it didn't give me much of an argument for my patient. I felt like a rock climber slipping down a sheer face and looking for a toehold.

"So what's your thing?" I asked, hoping to find a grip somewhere. "I'm a sculptor," he replied. That was appropriate, I thought—a carver of rocks. This kid lived to carve stone, he told me. It was his mis-sion, his passion, his purpose for living. But when I asked about his most recent piece he suddenly got all vague on me. He wasn't real sure exactly what that would be. I asked when he'd completed his last work. He was uncertain about that too, and admitted it had been a while since he'd done any carving. In fact, it had been over six months—not that smoking dope had anything to do with it, as he hastened to assure me.

I suggested an experiment. He was simply to refrain from smoking any marijuana for three weeks, then come back to me. "That's all?" he queried. "Yep, that's it." He agreed to try it and left the office happily.

He returned in three weeks, as prescribed. He'd smoked no mari-juana, as agreed. So, had he seen any difference?, I wanted to know. He grinned sheepishly and pulled out two photos, one of a completed piece of sculpture, the other of a work in progress. Both had been done in the past three weeks, after a year of no work. "I guess smoking weed does have a bad effect on me," he admitted. I agreed. Marijuana is highly unlikely to kill you, but it can sure make you dopey and unmotivated if you use enough of it. He decided to limit his pot use to the occasional recreational/inspirational occasion and curtail the daily use which had rendered him a lump of clay.

Marijuana figured prominently in another one-session case, though I'd scarcely call it a success story. A woman consulted me about the problem she was having with her son's drug use. I asked her what the problem was. "He's smoking up all *my* dope!" she snorted. I told her I couldn't help her, but if she'd leave immediately I wouldn't charge her for the session. Sometimes even the obvious truth isn't enough, and I get tired of people who only want to change somebody else.

One-shot cures make good stories and make you feel like a wonderful therapist. Sometimes, however, they are downright inconvenient, not to mention bad for business. "D'Anthony" was a three-and-a-half-year-old nursery school student who was to be my semester project in a graduate psychology course. D'Anthony was the biggest, toughest, and smartest kid in his class and he took full advantage of it. If he wanted a toy, he grabbed it. If his classmate protested, D'Anthony slugged him and kept the toy. When the teacher tried to correct him, D'Anthony would throw dramatic and disruptive tantrums, rolling and kicking and screaming and swinging at anybody who dared approach too closely. For all practical purposes D'Anthony was running the day care. That's when they decided to call in the Law. I was the man with the badge, and I had a whole semester to clean up Dodge City.

Me and my trusty Deputy, that is, since I had an undergraduate student to assist me. I was to help design a behavioral treatment program and supervise her in implementing it. Our plan was to play with D'Anthony for a couple of weeks, both to observe his behavior and to establish ourselves as "reinforcers" or rewarding persons. Then we'd systematically use our attention to reward good behavior and remove ourselves to punish bad behaviors. It wasn't hard to build a relationship with D'Anthony, as he was bright, curious, affectionate, and playful. He took to us immediately, especially to me, since he had no father and was starved for male attention. He loved wearing my big black cowboy hat, which I extended to him as a special privilege for acting right. The project was going beautifully until I made the fatal mistake of telling D'Anthony what we were going to do:

"D'Anthony, you and I are buddies, and I like playing with you a lot. I like letting you wear my hat, and it looks good on you. But I don't like it when you hit the other kids. That makes me feel sad. So if you hit somebody I'm going to take my hat back for the rest of that day. I also don't like it when you roll around on the floor and scream and kick. When you do that, I'm going to stop playing with you and go home for that day. Do you understand?"

D'Anthony responded by casually punching the first kid who wandered into range. I removed the hat from his head and returned it to my own. D'Anthony threw himself at my feet, screaming and thrashing. I stepped over him and strode out the door, without saying a word. And that was it. For the remainder of the semester D'Anthony threw neither another punch nor another tantrum, what behaviorists call "one-trial learning." My project was ruined, and I had to rustle us up another patient. D'Anthony got to ride in my MG convertible to the ice cream store for a special treat.

D'Anthony taught me some important lessons about therapy. Never underestimate or patronize your patient, especially if he's a child. And the best behavior program is no substitute for a clear explanation and consistent enforcement of limits. Finally, be ready to alter your course at any moment. Sometimes the magic works even better than you could hope for.

CHAPTER SEVEN
Name That Tune

PSYCHOTHERAPY IS SUPPOSED TO BE based on a clear plan, developed from a solid analysis of the case and underpinned by a thorough understanding of psychological theory. In actual practice, it is often a stab-in-the-dark, hit-or-miss, fly-by-the-seat-of-your-pants operation. That's especially true of family therapy, where the issues are often too complex, the action too rapid and the relationship nuances too subtle to track it all at a conscious, rational level. Sometimes you are so caught up in listening to the music that you miss the lyrics altogether. That is, a family therapist must be constantly attuned not only to what people are saying, but to how they are saying it. That's because family therapy is all about relationships, and relationships are transacted largely by way of *nonverbal* communication. *How* you say something to another person defines the nature of your relationship with him. That's why wives get mad if their husbands "talk down" to them, why parents say to their kids, "Don't use that tone of voice with me, Buster," and why a husband will explain that he slugged his wife because she gave him "that look." In relationships the more important messages are not in the words but in how they are said. In a sense, then, it's the family therapist's job to "name that tune," then try to rewrite the score in a more functional manner.

So in family therapy the critical interventions and the therapeutic changes often occur at the nonverbal level, which means even the therapist may not know in words what has transpired or why her input has been helpful. A lot of the fancy case analyses found in professional books and journals are done entirely after the fact. At the time of the actual intervention, the therapist was relying on pure "feel." Appropriately, songs, which meld verbal to nonverbal communication, can be a way of bridging the gap between these levels of the message. Sometimes in therapy a song will come into my head and I'll recognize it as a meaningful comment on what is happening in the therapy. For example, I might think of Bonnie Raitt's line about not being able to have love if you're keeping score. I'll realize that the couple I'm working with are running a tab on what they do for each other instead of freely and lovingly giving of themselves. I'll comment on that, perhaps even by singing the line to them. I think of these songs as messages from my subconscious mind, and I've learned to trust their input.

I once got stuck seeing a family late in the evening, when they showed up at the mental health center in a crisis. A mother and two young teenagers, they came in bickering and fussing and arguing heatedly. They were so caught up in the blood-lust of battle that they barely noted my presence. Meanwhile, I was exhausted from a long day's work, didn't need their anger and chaos, and was frankly a bit mush-brained. I struggled to make sense of this frenzied dispute but I found myself with no clear idea of what it was all about. Everybody was attacking and counter-attacking and defending each other, and there seemed little consistency in who went after whom for what. Sister would attack Brother, let's say, and Mom would defend him, only to turn around seconds later and berate her son for something else. It really seemed utterly random and arbitrary, and I just wanted to go home.

Not knowing what else to do, and perhaps unconsciously trying to point out how crazy and absurd all this was, I began to jump in with my own random and capricious comments, directing them indiscriminately at one family member or another. I might scold one or support another, then reverse myself unpredictably and attack my former ally. I was surprised to find that the family readily accepted whatever I said, even though I obviously had no idea what I was talking about. Brother might complain that Sister always left clothes on the floor. "Yeah," I'd add, "and you always leave your shoes in the hall where people will trip over them." Brother would immediately back me up with, "That's right!" Or I'd defend Mom for being late, blaming it on Brother's refusal to empty the dishwasher. "You *never* empty the dishwasher," Sister would chime in. It was really kind of fun, in a bizarre, surrealistic way.

Then I began to notice that after my interventions (or interruptions) the family would seem to lose energy for a while. They'd get a little quieter, perhaps even pause briefly before taking up the next line of attack. While they were highly skilled at their angry three-person interactions, it appeared they were not so adept at a four-man game. So I kept intervening with my nonsensical comments, and gradually they calmed down some. I began to wonder how they'd handle a very simple two-person quarrel, with no one running to the defense of either combatant. So I began cutting off the third person before he or she could enter the fray. "Hey, let's just watch those two fight," I'd whisper. "This ought to be good." And that person and I would sit out the next round. Sure enough, they couldn't play a two-party game, either! They just kept winding down.

I continued to start them up and let them run down for about an hour, until finally the four of us sat there in breathy silence. It was as if the plutonium rods had been spent and the reactor core had burned itself out. "Anybody got anything more to say?" Nobody did. I sent them home quietly, with instructions to see me in a week. Other than a vague awareness of a nasty divorce, I had no idea what their problem was or why they came in.

They had a pretty good week, with much less conflict and uproar. I finally began to receive a few sketchy details on what was going on. There had indeed been an ugly divorce, with Dad abandoning the family for a high-living, low-class floozy, leaving them destitute. Mom was trying to finish her nurse's training and earn enough to support them as a hotel night clerk. Brother and Sister were so hurt and scared and angry they literally were pulling knives on each other. Interestingly, though their fighting often escalated to this dangerous level of violence, neither of them ever really got hurt. Further, they complained bitterly, each of them, that the other was constantly bugging them. "She's always coming in my room, messing with my stuff." "He won't leave me alone, playing my radio and talking to me when I'm trying to study." It occurred to me that despite their angry complaints, each was actually seeking to spend time with the other! They couldn't do it nicely because they were so hurt and angry, but they loved and needed each other badly. So I gave them a nice, hostile excuse to be together.

I set up a program in which whenever one sibling came uninvited into the other's room, the other was entitled to spend ten minutes in the first one's room. I told the brother, "If she touches *your* things in *your* room, you get to bug her for ten minutes in *hers*." "Yeah," he agreed. "That'll fix her." And she got ten minutes in his place whenever he annoyed her in her own. She loved it. I sent them out gleefully contemplating the time they'd spend bothering each other, knowing that they needed each other's company but had to have an angry, face-saving way to get it.

I never did find out exactly what they'd come in for or thought their problem was. I did run into the mother several months later, in the hospital where she was a student nurse. She told me they were all getting along fine and asked me for a letter of reference, which I was happy to provide.

The two great determinants of human personality are genetics and early upbringing, both of which mean "family." Who we are is so intertwined with our membership in a family that it is impossible to truly know someone without at least some understanding of his or her family. Family is the background music that provides the context for everything we are, everything we do. Every family has its own traditions, customs, and habits that are passed from each generation to the next, patterns of behavior difficult to escape from. For example, the first sex offender I worked with was a fifteen-year-old boy who'd been caught messing with his little sister. When I asked where he'd gotten the idea to do such things, he answered that he'd seen his father having sex with his older sister. We traced sexual abuse through at least four and probably five generations of that middle-class Midwestern family. At least three males had actually been imprisoned for it. My patient was simply upholding the family tradition. When I see a case of child sexual abuse I always look elsewhere in the family to see if there is more. I'm rarely disappointed. I've seen women who were raped by every man and boy in the family, just as their sisters and mothers were.

Families are very protective of their own ways, even inappropriate or criminal ones. Again, incest is a prime example. I saw a family in which all the girls were molested. No one talked about it, but everyone knew that when Mother told them to "be nice to Uncle Joe," she meant they should perform oral sex on him. When my patient, a young woman, revealed that Uncle Joe and Grandpa had both molested her, she was branded a liar and ostracized by the whole family. When her cousin came forward and confirmed her story with similar allegations, she too was turned out of the family, which rallied instead around Uncle Joe. Nowhere is "blaming the victim" so common as in incest. I've seen many victims who told their mothers what was happening, only to be punished, called a "slut," and told it was their fault. That's if the mother believed them at all. Ironically, children are taught in school to inform a parent if someone is touching them inappropriately. Yet the most likely perpetrator is dear old Dad himself, often with the collaboration and cooperation of his sweet wife.

It is these *patterns* of family interaction that family therapists see as the root of most psychological problems. The real pathology is in the way family members relate to each other. Who actually becomes symptomatic and shows up as the "patient" is somewhat arbitrary, and she may even be the healthiest one in the family. The "depressed" adolescent described in Chapter Six, for example, was a sign of a deeper marital problem in the family. His parents' conflict with each other prevented them from dealing effectively with their son's problem. Or, viewed from a different perspective, the teenager's problem served the purpose of keeping his conflicted parents together. Similarly, "school phobia" appears to represent a fearful child, one who is afraid to leave Mother and go off to school. But the real phobic is Mom, who is afraid to let go of her baby and stay home alone. It is *mutual* "separation anxiety" with the child and mother clinging dependently to each other. Dad is usually very distant and uninvolved, which is why Mother clings to her only companion, the child. Her own dependency needs prevent the mother from effectively disciplining her child and resolving the problem.

This is a subtype of a pathological family pattern called "enmeshment," in which individuals are *too* close to each other. It is also found in anorexics, who are very phobic little girls (or, infrequently, boys). In enmeshed families everybody is over-involved with everybody else. I saw an anorexic family in which the mother checked daily on the success or failure of everybody's bowel movements, even Dad's. If I asked the patient how she felt, Mom would answer, "She feels fine" or, "She's unhappy." The boundaries between individuals become blurred in such families, leading to great confusion and poor self-images. In fact, this kind of intrusive enmeshment is thought to lead to the development of Borderline Personality Disorder, in addition to all sorts of psychosomatic illnesses.

The ultimate in enmeshment, however, was a mother and teenaged daughter I worked with in Austin. Elaborately garbed in identical hippie beads and bandana-wrapped Afros, these two bounced bralessly into my office and tried to sit in the same chair. (Remember, this was about 1974.) "Kami Sue" was barely out of her own adolescence chronologically, and not at all behaviorally or emotionally. "Kami Two" was only fifteen, but looked and sounded considerably older. They looked like twin sisters and acted like buddies, not parent and child. I had trouble telling them apart, and, it quickly became evident, so did they! Each would answer for the other, complete the other's sentences, and describe the other's feelings as if her own. They sometimes became confused as to who thought or felt what.

"Kami Two's been horribly depressed," said her mother, "She can't sleep or eat and has terrible nightmares."

"No, Mother, you're the one with the nightmares; I'm just worried about school," countered her daughter.

The air was thick with madness, and I began to feel my own contact with reality getting a little tenuous.

The reason for this craziness, and Kami Two's distress, soon became clear. She and Kami Sue shared *everything*. There were no secrets, no boundaries, no generation gaps. Their individual personalities blended and merged into one amorphous super-amoebic blob. They shared the same clothes, the same hairdo, the same bedroom. They shared the same hookah to smoke dope with. They even shared the same boyfriends, as Kami Sue had shared her daughter with a long string of lovers. No wonder Kami Two seemed so mature, yet had such a vague sense of self that she couldn't tell where she ended and her mom started. At some level she knew this relationship and lifestyle were crazy, and this was the source of her distress.

Kami Two's existential agony was beautifully revealed in a dream (once we sorted out that it was in fact her dream and not her mother's). She was crossing a parched and endless desert, seemingly with no hope of survival. She had struggled for ages, it seemed, treading across shifting, swirling mountains of sand, when she came upon a large Bedouin tent. Entering, she found it empty except for a Persian rug on which a coffin sat. As she approached it with a sense of dread, and yet with curiosity, a skeletal baby girl leaped from the coffin and landed on her chest. The infant clung to her desperately, digging her claws into Kami Two's flesh and palpably sucking the life out of her. "That baby is me!" she raged at her mother. "You have stolen my childhood and even my identity. I have no life, no self of my own." And she was right. Her mother had turned her into a Borderline Personality like herself, and at the heart of this disorder is a profound identity diffusion.

Observing the patterns of families in therapy is very like tuning in to the themes and subthemes in a symphony. Melodies weave in and out and reoccur with subtle and complex variations. You see this melodic patterning in families, too, and it often points to the underlying problem to be addressed. For example, a pediatrician and I collaborated on the case of "Tommy," the adopted son of a young professional couple. Tommy was failing first grade and his behavior was disruptive and unacceptable. My evaluation indicated Tommy had ADHD, and the pediatrician identified a visual problem. Ritalin and eyeglasses helped tremendously, and Tommy was soon out of danger academically. But his behavior continued to be a problem, both at home and at school. Most seriously, his tendency towards light-fingeredness was actually getting worse.

We had only the sketchiest information on Tommy's pre-adoption history, but it was known that he'd been severely neglected and physically abused. Thus, it wasn't surprising that he was angry, defiant, self-injurious, and passive-aggressive. But he'd been adopted nearly three years earlier. Why was he stealing things now, and why was his theft accelerating? We knew Tommy stole from his parents, teachers, and classmates whenever he was angry or felt he'd been treated unfairly. How did this behavior pattern fit into that of his family?

The answer became clear when his mother, who came from a very well-to-do family, was arrested for shop-lifting a tube of lipstick. Exploring this behavior in family sessions, it gradually appeared that Mother had done this before, always when she was angry at Tommy's dad. Dad, a promising young attorney, was embarrassed and enraged at his wife's criminal misconduct. His public humiliation and the threat to his career were her passive-aggressive way to express her anger (for she dared not confront him openly). Tommy's stealing, while no doubt primed by his history of abuse and facilitated by ADHD impulsivity, was also a variation on a family interaction pattern. The focus of therapy shifted to assertiveness training and anger management, and *everybody* was invited to participate.

(This case was published with several others in "Family Therapist and Pediatrician: Teaming Up on Four Common Behavioral Pediatrics Problems" by Frey and Wendorf, in *Family Systems Medicine*, 1984.)

It is uncanny at times how families transmit their behavior patterns through succeeding generations. Sons of alcoholics become alcoholics, and daughters grow up to marry alcoholics, both winding up in the same sick marriage their parents endured. Mothers who binge and purge produce daughters who starve themselves, and children of divorce are at high risk to be divorced themselves. Victims go on to become perpetrators in an endless "Cycle of Abuse." The route of transmission is often subtle, even purposely concealed, yet children perceive and emulate these family interaction patterns quite unconscious of why they are doing it. Some years back I made a rare home visit to a family with several children. At one point in the family session the parents asked their five-year-old son to excuse himself, as it was necessary to discuss the "family secret," and it was something he should not hear. The lad was most indignant, demanding he be allowed to continue with the rest of the family. It wasn't fair to exclude him, he declared, and besides, he already knew the family secret anyway. "No you don't," argued the parents; "Yes, I do," insisted the son. The parents refused to back down, and forced him to leave, but as he did this five-year-old loudly proclaimed, "The family secret is my big sister is a bastard." The parents were horrified and amazed, not only to hear such language from their young son, but because he was, of course, quite correct. His older sister had indeed been conceived out of wedlock, before the parents' marriage, a "secret" they'd tried to cover up for fifteen years. How could he know this?, they asked.

"I've always known it; so has everyone else in the family," he replied.

Family therapists know that there truly are few, if any, "family secrets," though it may take longer for some to emerge than for others. The presenting problem in this family was the fifteen-year-old daughter sneaking out at night to see her boyfriend, then lying about it. "Patterns."

Are we doomed, then, simply to repeat the patterns we grow up with? Is our family an inescapable part of our "karma?" No; enlightenment and release are possible. We are all ultimately responsible for our own lives and our own behavior, however compelling the family's traditions may be. If I didn't believe that, I couldn't be a therapist. And over the years I've seen both horrid, sociopathic children produced by good, loving families and wonderful human beings emerge from sick, evil ones. Even the Jeffrey Dahmers, Ted Bundys, and Charles Mansons of the world must have received *some* nurturing, or they'd not have survived their infancy.

On the other hand, Birmingham celebrity Shelley Stewart saw his father murder his mother, then literally grew up on the street, living in abandoned cars, chicken coops, and foster homes. His brother, a heroin addict, died in prison. But Shelley never missed a day of school, ultimately putting himself through college and becoming a radio and TV personality. He was the first African American to own a radio station in Alabama, and he now heads a large advertising agency. And he's a nice guy. In the long run you can write your own song if you really try. Still, don't be too surprised if the melodic line sounds just a little like your mother's lullaby.

The task of the family therapist is not only to help you name the tune (identify the dysfunctional interaction patterns) but to help you rewrite the song. How to do that varies enormously from case to case and taxes the imagination and ingenuity of the most creative therapists, though here, too, there are some recognizable patterns. Sometimes it's enough to relabel the tune, thereby making it one the family is familiar with handling. Relabeling adolescent depression as "rebellion" puts it squarely in the father's realm of expertise, enabling him to resolve an otherwise mysterious malady. Conversely, diagnosing (relabeling) Dad's lack of energy and interest in his family as "depression" turns him from an irresponsible person into a "sick" one, points to an effective treatment (Prozac), and encourages his family to relate to him in a mutually rewarding and loving fashion. Unless he truly is a rotten guy, most fathers will become more energized, more involved, and more affectionate in response.

Sometimes the therapist ignores the lyrics and rewrites the tune, perhaps just re-orchestrating it as described above with the fighting brother and sister. Sometimes you can change people's behavior, even their sense of self, just by having them dress differently. Thus, I had a college student dress up in a business suit to confront her parents about their continuing tendency to treat her like a baby. Not only did the parents respond to her differently, she reported that she even felt more grown-up herself. Other times the pattern is so engrained the only way to change it is to exaggerate it. It's a kind of reverse psychology run amok, capitalizing on the paradoxical nature of living, especially human beings. It's an odd fact of life that one must sometimes approach change by accentuating the status quo. The best way to release excess muscle tension, for example, is to tense the muscles even more tightly. When you let go, your muscles slide on past their original level of tension and become more relaxed. This technique is a standard in stress management and can even be used as a hypnotic induction. Similarly, to stop hyperventilation you can hold your breath, breathe into a bag, or force yourself to breathe faster. Family therapists often help people change by advising them to do more of the same—sometimes much more.

For example, a mother (the lady who lost 100 pounds for me) was ashamed and worried about her interaction with her daughter concerning the child's grades. Every six weeks her twelve-year-old would trudge homeward to present a scorecard full of Cs and Ds, and every six weeks Mom would erupt in volcanic fury. She knew this was inappropriate and harmful to the girl. Further, it not only didn't help, it encouraged the lass to blame her academic problems on her bitchy mother instead of taking responsibility herself. It actually motivated her to continue to fail, in passive-aggressive retribution against her mom. But Mom didn't know how to change. She'd tried restraining herself, but she just couldn't resist. That's fine, I suggested; don't resist. In fact, do it *more*. She was confused.

"Do it *more*," I said. "When your daughter hands you her report card, I want you to go totally psycho. Scream, cry, tear your clothing. Roll on the floor. I want you to go so thoroughly nuts that your daughter realizes it's too much to be real, that you're faking it."

Mom recognized that this advice was nuts, but the challenge of the charade appealed to her. "Can you do that?" I asked. "I can sure have fun trying," she replied.

And she did. She screamed, yelled, hollered, ranted, raved, and carried on hysterically. She rolled on the floor and jumped on the table and said ridiculous things. Her daughter stared at her, first in amazement, then terrified, then horrified, then confused, then finally bemused. Mom had lost it! She was just as whacked out as the daughter had always believed! Finally Mom could no longer control herself. The look on her daughter's face was simply too marvelous to ignore. She collapsed in a giggling, chortling, then guffawing heap, tears of laughter rolling down her cheeks. The daughter, seeing through the game and recognizing an Oscar-level performance, also burst into laughter and tears. The two of them rolled on the floor together, laughing and crying and hugging until they ached. Then they got up and had a quiet talk about the grade situation, agreeing on set homework hours and a plan for tutoring. The pattern was broken and the problem was solved, at least for the moment.

The challenge for the therapist is to find the right intervention for the right family at the right time. I tried the same maneuver on a father-son combo, but both lacked the sense of humor and sense of drama to pull it off. When these two escalated, it was to suicide, runaway, and car theft. They needed a whole different tune and maybe a different band leader than me.

CHAPTER EIGHT
Truly Crazy People

FOR MOST OF MY CAREER, truly crazy people constituted only a small minority of my patients. ("Crazy" is not a technical term, but one commonly used by doctors and patients alike.) That's partly because I spent most of it in private practice, doing mostly outpatient work and seeing a lot of children and adolescents. It's partly because most truly crazy people either take their medicine and lead relatively normal lives, disappear from view and live under the viaduct, or bounce in and out of hospitals and prisons I don't visit. Truly crazy people are always sad to see, sometimes annoying as well, and often not very entertaining. Some are endearing, others hilarious. Some are fascinating for the creativity of their insanity. They are, all in all, mostly like all the rest of us, only maybe a bit more so. Over the years I've seen a few who were memorable indeed.

In psychiatric jargon, what most people would call crazy we call "psychotic." To be psychotic means to have lost contact with reality in some major way. Psychotic people have crazy, irrational ideas called "delusions," which have no basis in and conflict with reality. Singer Paul Simon describes someone smashing into a brick wall because he believes he has comic-book style supernatural powers. Delusions aren't just a matter of fooling yourself, as in believing you're exceptionally pretty or you can quit cocaine any old time. Delusions are wildly impossible, irrational ideas such as that one is actually Jesus

Christ returned or that one is controlled by a hostile conspiracy of alien invaders. Or, they might be even more interesting and outlandish, as in this excerpt from my actual psychological report on a young hospital patient:

"Portia was referred by her outpatient psychiatrist, Dr. James Barnett, who has been treating her since her release from some forty-eight days in Brookwood Hospital. I found Portia to be alert and well oriented, but hyperactive, if not hypomanic, immature, and at times grossly inappropriate. She recognizes some of the changes in herself, stating that she feels younger and that she has lost part of herself and recognizing that her former thinking was delusional. At the time of her hospitalization, she thought that her father was Jeffrey Dahmer, her mother was Elton John, her boyfriend was stalking her for cocaine, the F.B.I was after her, her coach was taping her, her sister was Eve and her brother-in-law Adam. She also states that at the time she heard voices talking to her when no one was present, these auditory hallucinations being the voices of Chelsea Clinton and Prince William of England. She states that the voices told her that they were going to kill her, that she was dead, and that she should do crazy things. During that time she became quite paranoid, feeling that she was being stalked and would be attacked, and she lost a great deal of weight and slept very little."

Psychotic people can't distinguish between internal and external stimuli, so that their own thoughts sound to them like real voices from outside, or they "see" faces that actually exist only in their imagination. These visions and voices are called "hallucinations," and they are pathognomonic of psychosis. That is, their existence *names* the pathology as psychosis. It is also possible to have tactile (touch) or olfactory (smell) hallucinations, as well as auditory or visual ones. The different symptoms have diagnostic value, in fact, since schizophrenic patients tend towards auditory and perhaps visual hallucinations, while victims of acute brain injury or illness are more likely to experience olfactory ones. These false sensations are typically pretty gross, such as the smell of excrement, spoiled food, or rotting flesh. In any case, truly psychotic (as opposed to merely weird) people mostly get that way through some kind of physical illness of the brain. It's possible just to get so stressed out that you "go nuts," but it's highly unlikely without a genetic predisposition. Most psychosis is due to schizophrenia, bipolar disorder (manic-depressive illness), or the use of hallucinogenic drugs. We'll take a look at some of each. Meantime, we should note that these psychoses have other symptoms, too, including mood disorders such as mania or depression, thought disorders such as incoherent or nonsequential speech, social isolation, and bizarre or disorganized behavior such as not bathing or sitting mute for days. It's even possible to be diagnosed with a psychosis without any delusions or hallucinations at all. And we're not talking about the "delirium" of a high fever or the forgetfulness and mental confusion which make up the "dementias" such as Alzheimer's.

Schizophrenia has been known of, and poorly understood, for a long time, but only recognized as a mental illness since the 1850s. The name, which means a splitting of the mind, was invented by Eugen Bleuler in 1911. It is *not* the same as Multiple Personality Disorder, in that the mind is not split into several personalities, as in MPD, but is split off from reality itself. We are now pretty confident that schizophrenia, or at least the tendency to develop it, is genetically inherited (whereas MPD is a post-traumatic disorder). There are several overlapping variants of the disease, but the most common is paranoid schizophrenia. In this version the patient has delusional ideas either of grandiosity ("I'm Jesus Christ") or persecution ("The Martians are out to get me"). These aren't so different as they sound, by the way: if there's a grand conspiracy to get you, then you must be pretty important ("They're trying to hang me on a cross *because* I'm the Messiah").

The definition of psychosis depends heavily on what is considered to be "reality" or at least "normality." Depending on what century you are born into, the same exact symptoms will get you exorcised for demonic possession, canonized a saint, burned as a witch, incarcerated in a snake pit, or medicated with Haldol. Take Joan of Arc, for example, the Patron Saint of France. She believed she heard the voice of God commanding her to lead an army and retake the Crown for the Dauphin. And she did just that, grandiose as it seems, though at the cost of her own martyrdom. Today she'd be hospitalized, given an MMPI (a self-administered questionnaire, the Minnesota Multiphasic Personality Inventory is the most widely used and most valid indicator of personality types), medicated with an anti-psychotic and sent on to a half-way house. Actually, even today it is sometimes possible to see visions or hear voices and be believed. A little girl visiting Alabama from the former Yugoslavia created an international sensation and brought thousands of pilgrims to a cotton field in Shelby County, Alabama, where she claimed to have received several visits from the Virgin Mary. Perhaps it was her simple nature and her obvious piety that turned the trick. It may also have been fortunate for her that she received her visions in the South, where such things are more likely to be taken at face value. I recently interviewed a candidate for the ministry, who told me he literally "heard" the voice of God, telling him to become a preacher. He heard it like I heard my kids yelling at each other. Yet, he's aware this is generally considered in our society to be crazy, and he has no other indications of psychosis. On the MMPI he came out as normal as a cheeseburger, and I passed him on to the Bishop.

Of course, you're not paranoid if people are truly out to get you, and sometimes it's hard to tell for sure. I saw a woman who believed the Mafia was out to do her in. That's believable, as I understand the Mafia are occasionally inclined towards that sort of behavior. What *wasn't* believable was that they'd mess with a small-potatoes nuisance like my patient or that professional hit men could be so inept as to leave her breathing. With my friend Dr. James Barnett, I treated an adolescent with the odd name of Tortellini (especially odd for a black kid) who believed he was a tornado and went whooshing about the unit. We were pretty sure he was truly psychotic. But an Austin State Hospital legend spoke of a patient who was obviously psychotic, hearing voices and going on boastfully about his ranches and oil wells and such. The staff humored him good-naturedly until the million-dollar checks started coming in. Even rich people get sick sometimes, and vice versa.

Many schizophrenics are aware that they are "crazy" at times; indeed that's one of the most frightening aspects of the illness. Imagine not being able to trust your own thoughts or perceptions because you know they play falsely with you. Many schizophrenics are quite intelligent, even though psychotic, and can appear perfectly sane for extended periods—until they begin describing their abduction by aliens from another galaxy. Or is alien abduction a *fact* that society irrationally refuses to accept? Some psychiatrists report hearing so many of these abduction tales and being so struck by the similarities in them that they are persuaded that they are literally true. How can we know for sure?

My brother Don treated a patient at Central State in Nashville who believed he was controlled by professors at Vanderbilt, via a radio receiver in his brain. This was hard to believe, not because university professors aren't a malicious lot who'd do that sort of thing, but because Vandy is a liberal arts school, where the technology probably isn't up to this kind of control. He'd get better and be released, returning to his family and his job. But eventually he'd begin to trust people enough to let them in on his little secret. They'd call in the authorities and he'd be hauled off to the hospital again. One day he told my brother, "You know, Doc, this time when I get out I'm not gonna tell anyone about the radio waves from Vanderbilt, and maybe they won't lock me up again." Don said, "Buddy, you're cured," and let him go home. It was the man's last admission, though he was probably still technically crazy. Another of Don's patients actually did believe he'd been abducted by aliens and recounted a fantastic galaxy-hopping voyage in a starship. He recalled a series of harrowing interstellar adventures and described bizarre alien life forms, until Don interrupted him and accurately completed the narrative for him. The man was utterly amazed and a little frightened at the clairvoyance of his Shrink, until Don explained he'd seen it all on Star Trek. Only then did this man see the connection and realize how he'd woven a TV show into his own delusional schema.

The link between genius and insanity is well established in legend and lore and receives some validation from scientific research. Patients with Bipolar Disorder, for example, are often exceptionally creative and brilliant people. Vincent Van Gogh is a good example from history. He suffered from terrible bouts of depression, as well as wild manic episodes. He cut off his ear and sent it to his lover, then painted a haunting self-portrait with his head in a bandage. The link between psychosis and religious insight also demands closer examination and is receiving it from a new group of self-styled "neurotheologians." As reported in *Newsweek*, these neuroscientists have used brain scans to determine that Zen Buddhist monks achieve a brain state during meditation in which the part of the brain which distinguishes between internal and external realities is suddenly quieted. Zen calls this state of consciousness "satori" or spiritual awakening. Enlightened ones describe the experience as a profound sense of connection with the ultimate essence of the Universe. The distinction between Self and Other is lost and one's own soul is seen as sharing in the Universal Soul. One is aware of the true nature of his "Buddha self." The scientists note that this state of consciousness seems to be hard-wired into our brains, as if it encapsulates a genetic memory of ancient encounters with God, or at least serves as God's reminder that he is our Creator. They see it as the source of profound religious experiences. Certainly, spiritual seekers have used meditation for thousands of years as the royal pathway to enlightenment. What is interesting is that this state of consciousness can also be achieved by the use of hallucinogenic drugs, by way of ritual and repetition, even by way of sexuality, all of which have their own long-standing religious traditions. Users of LSD describe a similar sense of the oneness of all creation, including themselves. Are we in some way hard-wired to perceive God? An old NOVA program, on PBS, documented cases of patients with temporal lobe epilepsy who either believed themselves to be God or experienced intense religious experiences in connection with their seizures. The neurologist treating these patients hypothesized that their intense religious experiences had to do with the flood of feelings they received due to the spontaneous activation of nerve cells associated with emotion. He noted that it is the emotion attached to a sensation that renders it meaningful to us and described a brain-damaged patient who did not believe his parents were truly who they claimed to be, even though they looked and sounded exactly like his "real" parents. His problem was that the emotional centers of his brain had been damaged, so the sight of his parents was unaccompanied by any emotional reaction, and therefore it seemed meaningless to him. He concluded they must be imposters. The epilepsy patients, on the other hand, experienced intense emotion in connection with *everything* they perceived, and they experienced this as a spiritual connection to the Cosmos itself. It is troubling to note that this loss of the distinction between internal and external realities, between one's own thoughts and the voices of others, between meaningful emotional experience and false reality is precisely the defining characteristic of psychosis. How then does one distinguish between genuine religious insight and the psychotic rambling of a mentally ill or brain-injured person? It's a question of historic significance, and nobody's got a clear answer yet. It is also a question of great importance in the diagnosis and treatment of psychosis.

My own second-favorite schizophrenic patient was "Mary," the British-born wife of the upholsterer who redid the interior of an old Jaguar with me. Mary was a sweetheart and would always have tea and cookies for me when I came to check on the car's headliner (mohair, of course) or the door panels (lovely red leather all new-smelling and grand). Then Mary would forget to take her meds and would end up on the roof, screaming almost unintelligibly in harsh, cockney accents. As nearly as I could tell, she believed she was under siege by Nazis and was holding them at bay from a machine-gun emplacement behind the chimney. Mary was a redhead and when she got acutely psychotic her green eyes would blaze like a couple of signal flares. She was harmless, as the machine-gun was just as hallucinatory as the storm-troopers, and she would soon yield to the persuasions of her husband and me. She'd resume taking her medication and shortly be as right as the rain in Spain again. It was the cookies I found so endearing, but I'll never forget the emerald fire in Mary's eyes.

My favorite schizophrenic patient was "Gilberto," a young Mexican-American musician I treated at the mental health center in

Austin. Our acquaintance began when Stella, the receptionist, buzzed to inform me that my two o'clock intake had to be seen in the parking lot. Though I don't usually do drive-thrus, Gilberto's brothers escorted me to their car, where he was sitting like a slab of granite in the back seat. He stared straight ahead, heedless of my introduction, and said not a word. He wasn't angry or hostile or resistant or deaf, but he never turned his head or opened his mouth. I took his hand to shake it, and he left it hanging in air when I let go. Gilberto was obviously catatonic, the hallmark of an acute and very severe psychotic reaction.

As I made arrangements to admit Gilberto to the state hospital, his family related what they knew of his recent activities. He had gone to confession several times, apparently still troubled by some inappropriate "touching" when he was an altar boy. While his confession seemed to help at first, he had gotten increasingly distressed and agitated later, perhaps because seeing the priest had resurrected old memories and feelings. He'd begun talking excitedly about his "mission from God," though he was very confused as to what it might be. The rest of the story came from the Texas Highway Patrol: Gilberto had driven up I-35 until he ran out of gas, then gotten out and started walking. A trooper had found him trudging dazedly along, forty miles from his abandoned car. He'd mumbled something about being a disciple and how the Bible said "the disciples walked from town to town." Then he'd sat rigid and totally silent, just as I'd seen him. In Judea the next town is a few miles away; in Central Texas it may be a hundred.

Gilberto spent only three weeks in the hospital and showed up on time for his first follow-up with me. He was understandably shaken and puzzled by his strange misadventure, but was fairly happy and not at all psychotic. His memory of his psychotic episode was pretty vague, perhaps partly due to his use of marijuana. He had little insight into the cause of his breakdown but did realize that being molested had raised issues about his sexuality that he found troubling. He'd had what Freud called a "homosexual panic." So we set to work trying to sort all this out.

Gilberto was both easy and difficult to work with. A chunky, slightly pock-marked man with hair like black straw, he was extremely friendly and jovial. He had a good attitude about life and about himself, taking neither too seriously. For example, after hearing him play at several local dance halls, I observed that he was always accompanied by at least one and usually two or more gorgeous women. Considering this exceptional, even for a country-rock-Tejano "star," I commented on it, noting that he wasn't really the best-looking guy in town.

"I'm ugly, Bob," was his reply.

"Whoa, Gilly, I wouldn't say *that*," I countered, afraid I'd damage his self-esteem.

"Don't knock being ugly, man," he chuckled. "It's the best thing that ever happened to me. Actually, the girls love it." I couldn't argue with him, having seen the proof myself.

On the other hand Gilberto (or "Gilly," his stage name) required a bit of special handling. While he always greeted me from the stage at shows or dances, he was uncomfortable coming to the mental health center. So I agreed to meet him at restaurants, and we conducted his therapy over lunch—Dutch treat, of course. This would likely be considered unethical today, as it bordered on a social rather than professional relationship. So would going to hear him play music and sharing a beer at his breaks. But Gilberto felt respected and cared for and would likely have dropped out of therapy if forced to come to my office. Besides, I frequented the same honky-tonks and dance halls he did. Meanwhile, being Chicano, Gilberto knew all the best Tex-Mex restaurants, the ones that hadn't gotten discovered, appropriated, and ruined by Gringos. So the arrangement worked well for both of us.

The other problem we had was with his medication. This was the mid-'70s when the main line treatment for schizophrenia was the older phenothiazines like Mellaril and Thorazine. While these drugs were a revolutionary breakthrough that nearly emptied the state hospitals and saved millions from a horrible life, they also tended to have some unpleasant side effects. Gilberto complained that he felt as if enshrouded in a cottony cloud. He was sane, but as if one step removed from the world around him. This wasn't helpful in playing the Texas two-step. Further, the medication left him with the stiffness of limbs once known as the "Thorazine shuffle." Not good for a drummer, which was Gilberto's instrument. We switched meds several times, but he couldn't tolerate any of them and eventually decided to take his chances without any anti-psychotic. Fortunately Gilberto turned out to be in the one-third of schizophrenics who will have one psychotic episode and no more, even without maintenance medication. Another third will do well only with medication and the last third will remain psychotic no matter what you give them. Gilberto was lucky.

I should also mention that Gilberto's habitual use of marijuana may have played some role in precipitating his psychotic episode. Marijuana is ordinarily a very mild and not very dangerous drug. However, if your grip on reality is already a bit tenuous, marijuana can lead to a kind of real "reefer madness." I've seen it happen to several people, including an old friend who spent several days in his own personal Hell, believing the Devil was out to get him. What these individuals seemed to have in common was a rigidity of thought that could tolerate no ambiguity. They all seemed incredibly calm and solid, but this placid facade was hiding an inner turmoil. Marijuana distorted their perceptions just enough to create a psychotic panic. Gilly couldn't tolerate the thought that he might be gay. My friend said the distortion of time perception common to the marijuana "high" was simply too frightening for him to manage. He never tried it again. On the other hand, Gilberto continued to smoke pot regularly, without apparent ill effect.

The second easiest way to become psychotic is to inherit Bipolar Disorder, formerly known as Manic-Depressive Illness or Psychosis. As the name implies, bipolar disorder involves a cycling between episodes of mania and deep depression. The depressed part is obvious and known to most of us in milder form. Mania is a period of enormous energy and elated or expansive mood. Manics may be intensely angry or intensely happy, but they're always intensely *something*. They can go for days without sleep and often feel invincible and omnipotent. Then, like the Paul Simon line, they slam into the brick wall of depression.

Bipolar disorder is primarily a mood problem, but in extreme cases the patient can become truly psychotic, especially during the manic phase. The psychosis is usually manifested in the form of grandiose delusional thinking, such as "believing I had supernatural powers." And since the person is manic, he or she usually acts out whatever the delusion suggests. One of my patients, believing she was a Wall Street billionaire, bought a brand-new Mercedes automobile during a manic spending spree. For cash. She actually was pretty well off financially, and when the manic episode was over she kept the car. It cost her her marriage, but I still think she came out ahead, as the husband was a louse, and the Mercedes was a dreamboat. Another patient, a conservative and docile accountant, was arrested in the middle of the night for running around naked and breaking into cars. He sheepishly explained that he was looking for beer, hoping to drink himself down a bit. Well, okay, that made some sense, but why in the nude? "I don't know, Doc, but it made sense at the time." Still another patient, this one a demure middle-class housewife and realtor, got busted tap-dancing on the hood of a police car, screaming obscenities at the lady cop inside. By the time I saw her at the hospital she had calmed down a lot but was still somewhat confused and unaccustomedly seductive. Believing her husband was plotting to kill her, she'd led him a merry chase, hopping planes all over the country. He'd finally tracked her down and collared her on a brief home-town layover. In two weeks she'd earned enough frequent-flyer miles to send them both to Europe, but they could no longer afford to go.

As the accountant's story suggests, self-medication, often with alcohol, is a frequent complication of bipolar disorder, and not unheard of with schizophrenia. If you're a little too hyper, a couple of beers seems just the ticket to calm you down. On the depressed end, Scotch can look like a nice pick-me-up. Thus, alcoholism is frequently a comorbid condition for bipolar disorder. Less commonly, other drug abuse can either precipitate or result from a manic episode, which brings us 'round to good ole "Dwayne." Dwayne—which he pronounces "*Dee-wayne*"—suffers from bipolar disorder and an inordinate fondness for crack cocaine. Dwayne's a pretty hyper guy by nature and hardly needs a stimulant. When he's manic he orbits just low enough to graze the outer stratosphere. Yet Dwayne craves the pipe, knowing full well it will launch him on a parabolic arc which inevitably terminates with a crash landing in the County lock-up. Then he'd call me.

I often wouldn't actually *see* Dwayne for several years, but I'd hear from him whenever he was in trouble. He isn't hard to recognize, with his rapid-fire, high-pressured falsetto vice. Dwayne's voice cannot be adequately represented with the printed word, but my kids used to recognize him immediately (when he's manic; he's more subdued when depressed). "Dad, it's good ole Dwayne on the phone. I think he's in jail again." Try to imagine a particularly breathy piccolo, played at teletype speed, but with a plaintive, desperate undertone.

"Doctor Bob, it's me, Dwayne. It's me Doctor Bob. Doctor Bob you gotta help me. I need to go to the hospital, Doctor Bob. You can talk to the Judge and tell him to put me in Rehab, Doctor Bob. I wanna be committed, Doctor Bob. You're the best doctor in the world and I love you, man. If you had been my father I'd never been in this trouble. I love you, Doctor Bob. I love you, man."

He'd usually call me at home, and my then teenaged sons (who always answered the phone) would come squealing, "It's *Dee*-Wayne, Doctor Bob; he loves you and you gotta help him, Doctor Bob." I'd groan and ask him where he was.

"I'm at County, Doctor Bob. You gotta help me, Man. I love you, Doctor Bob . . ." I was able once to talk a judge into transferring Dwayne to Rehab and I'll probably regret it for the rest of my life. Dwayne thought I could do anything.

Dwayne's basket has a few cracked eggs even at his best; when he's manic he becomes totally scrambled. Dwayne's a compulsive Bible reader, and when he gets psychotic he has a hard time separating himself from its narrative. He's a prophet with a burning bush in his head, seeing signs of imminent doom. He's the Messiah, called upon to testify, sanctify, and condemn. He carries on lengthy conversations with his deceased brother and literally wrestles with the Devil in his cheap hotel room. Dwayne's also a recovering alcoholic and a four-time divorcee, but he's celibate and sober now, as he's "entered into a spiritual war." He's a gentle but simple soul, and he does genuinely love and respect me. I can't help liking him despite his relatively high nuisance value. I just wish I could keep him off the rock. I haven't heard from Dwayne in some years now and I can't say I miss him much, but I wish him well.

Lacking a genetic predisposition for schizophrenia or bipolar disorder, you can still make yourself truly crazy with drugs. Alcohol can do it, but it requires years of dedicated effort. Marijuana can do it, but only in rare cases like those described above and only temporarily. The fast track to drug-induced psychosis is by way of amphetamines ("speed") or hallucinogens such as "acid." Acid, or LSD, was the route selected by "Alice," one of the spookiest, most troubled, craziest, and most loveable adolescents I've ever worked with.

Alice was referred initially because she was failing in school. There was also some relatively passive rebellion, such as staying out past curfew, but most of her misconduct consisted of impish pranks and simply not doing her schoolwork. She was a cute, funny, bubbly little girl of fifteen when I first met her, although she could also become terribly depressed, even suicidal at times. With blond hair and blue eyes, she could easily have been my daughter, and at times she seemed to think she was. Her parents had tried everything they could think of, but Alice just kept trucking down her own highway. Alice and I hit it off immediately, though for no really discernible reason. Maybe it was the crooked way she grinned or her quirky sense of humor, or her mischievous playfulness. Like the Cindy Lauper song, Alice just wanted to have fun.

Yet there was also a dark side to Alice, a brooding, morbid tendency towards isolation and a preoccupation with death. That's what put her in the hospital the first time. And there was her continued academic failure. Psych testing showed that Alice was no Rhodes Scholar, but she was certainly bright enough to pass with only minimal effort. Her dad, a former vice cop, and her mom, a nurse, were concerned and cooperative with her treatment. But as we set and enforced tougher limits, Alice only escalated her misbehavior. Another suicide gesture led to another hospital stay, and her grades continued to be poor. Antidepressant medication didn't seem to be helping. In therapy Alice was engaging and entertaining and promised to do better, but wasn't really going anywhere. Something was missing, but we couldn't quite put our hands on it. And Alice was progressing from quirky to eccentric to downright strange, increasingly silly but also defiant. Nothing was making much sense, including Alice.

We knew Alice had tried smoking dope, but not enough to produce this clinical picture. Besides, she had tested clean for THC on the last two occasions. Then her dad found a little piece of ink blotter with tiny cartoon pictures on it and the puzzle quickly resolved itself. Alice was doing acid. In fact, as she later revealed, Alice was doing a *lot* of acid, dropping two or three hits a day for nearly two years! Unbelievably, she was using it at home, in her own room. Her parents didn't suspect this because they knew Alice was a weird kid anyway and because she kept her door shut and the stereo turned on. Besides, LSD had not shown up on the urine drug screens, which in those days were often not sensitive enough to pick up the minute traces of metabolites left behind from an acid trip.

At this point Alice was all but psychotic much of the time, not to mention suicidally depressed, so we put her back in the hospital and began the battle to recover her sanity. Alice had spent so much time in the hallucinogenic fantasy world of LSD that the universe occupied by the rest of us seemed drab and mundane to her. School was a bore, friends were a drag, and even her acid-metal-rock music wasn't exciting enough until drug-enhanced. She had used so much acid she was now experiencing almost constant "flashbacks" and was essentially "tripping" without need for further ingestion of the drug. I knew we were in for a struggle when I sat next to her on the acute care unit and she suddenly looked upward and broke into her crooked, spaced-out, wild-eyed yet somehow beatific grin. "What are you doing Alice?" "Oh, just listening to the pretty colors," she smiled.

Alice was living in an alternate universe, and one more glamorous, exciting, and colorful than our own. How could I lure her back to reality? One drawing card was her family. For all her rebelliousness, Alice loved her parents and appreciated how they'd stuck by her. She was particularly close to her father, a feeling she transferred to me, thereby giving me a therapeutic handhold on her. And there were boys. She liked boys, and she was cute, but most guys don't want to date Lucy in the Sky with Diamonds. We transferred her from the acute ward, filled mostly with geriatric dementia cases, to the adolescent unit, which had boys. She liked that. We spent a lot of time talking, mostly about how she could be happy and successful in the real world if she stayed away from her zombie medicine. And we kept her away from drugs. It was a real tug of war, but gradually we pulled Alice out of Dreamland and back down to Earth. The boys helped a lot.

So far as we could tell Alice stayed clean and sober for several years, and her flashbacks eventually dwindled away. She didn't finish high school, but did obtain a G.E.D. and a job, where she worked quite responsibly. She met a boy there and they married and moved to a nearby town, so I lost track of her for a while. When she did call me again she'd left her husband, who turned out to be an abusive, lazy, drug-addicted loser. She was back with her parents again, but had not come home empty-handed. Against all genetic odds, Alice and her mate had produced a perfectly lovely baby girl with the same dreamy blue eyes and crooked grin as her mother. And a good mother she was, though she had at least one drug relapse.

Of the thousands of patients I've seen, it's funny who I remember and what stands out about them. With these "crazy" people it's not so much their craziness as their other human qualities that make them memorable. I remember Mary's green laser eyes and machine guns and cookies. With Gilberto I recall his easy gratitude for being homely, and his lovely escorts. Then there's Dwayne of the falsetto "I love you, Dr. Bob" voice. Alice is unforgettable for listening to the colors, a funny grin—and a bow tie. When I *have* to wear a tie, it's always a bow tie and always a tie-it-yourself type. I've worn a long tie once in thirty years, when I lost a bet to a fellow therapist and had to wear his tie to the Adolescent Unit. So I passed out the wildest (bow) ties I owned and had the patients wear them to Group. The kids thought this was a kick, especially Alice. So she paid me back with a gift, which still sits on my bookshelf. It's the ugliest bow tie I have ever seen, and a clip-on to boot. She grinned as she gave it to me. "Here, listen to *these* colors."

CHAPTER NINE
The Merely Weird

THERE ARE OTHER PATIENTS WHO fall well short of meeting the diagnostic criteria for psychosis but are still decidedly strange. There was the guy who had sex with road-killed animals, then dissected their corpses. He also liked to have sex with his wife without waking her up (which I suspected might be her preference as well). There was the kid who squawked like a parrot, repeatedly saying, "I'm weird," while shrugging his shoulders and blowing some unknown substance off them. When the hospital staff forbade these behaviors he decided he was just "strikingly unconventional," a compromise saying we agreed to tolerate. There was "Southside Sallie," an eccentric street character from a well-to-do family and the only patient I've ever had to have forcibly ejected from my office. (She broke a window.) And Glenda, who didn't eat for six months and had surgery, losing 100 pounds, so I would fall in love with her. I remember Anna, a 65-pound anorexic who could barely walk when I met her and who stayed in the hospital for nine months rather than eat. As we talked one day, a new patient ambled slowly by, her emaciated frame supported by a rolling IV holder. I asked her how it made her feel to see such a weak and bony creature. "Jealous," said Anna. Who could forget "Artie," the 400-pound obsessive-compulsive who took such pride in his ability to "piss people off," or Walker, who would literally starve before he'd utter a word?

At a lesser intensity, I've seen people whose weirdness was limited to a single behavior or two, such as carving words into their skin or pulling out all their hair. I can tell how "Patty" is doing by whether she's just wearing a cap or has to have an entire wig to cover the bald spot. Patty is intelligent and a nice person, but her stress-management skills could stand some improvement, to say the least. Some of my favorites—since every doctor relishes an unsual case—are paranoid personalities, patients who are not psychotic but whose suspicions and mistrust are clearly exaggerated and unrealistic. Wilbur, for example, was convinced his dissertation committee was discriminating against him and conspiring with other faculty to deny him his doctoral degree—in psychology. He insisted on presenting his case in elaborate detail, showing me voluminous but vacuous documentation of their misdoing. Such paranoids are interesting because, generally speaking, they are bright and energetic and well-organized, yet completely illogical and unaware of their own mental processes. They beautifully exemplify the dynamic of "projection," a psychological defense mechanism in which one denies one's own emotion and projects it like a movie into the mind of another. Paranoids believe the world is hostile to them and out to get them, yet they are themselves extremely angry people. They are unable to accept their own hostility, so they see it as if it was coming from others. Eventually their accusations and ravings do engender hostility to them, which serves to validate their allegations of persecution, but they never realize that they made it happen themselves. They are very difficult to treat because even the slightest hint they might be wrong or causing their own distress is taken as a betrayal and an attack. The therapist is then seen as part of the conspiracy! When I suggested Wilbur might do better to be more diplomatic with his professors, he came charging into my waiting room, ranting about how I'd stabbed him in the back and threatening to retaliate with a malpractice suit. At that point I really did become angry at him.

Another paranoid patient mailed me a twenty-five page dossier (legal size, single spaced) detailing her "story of Fraud, Conspiracy,

Harassment, Invasion of Privacy, Treachery, Deceit, and Entrappment" (*sic*) at the hands of the police, the mental health authority, the FBI, her ex-husband, and most lawyers in the western hemisphere. It includes a letter, all full of Capitalizations and Underlined Words, addressed to a county commissioner, with copies sent to a list of people and agencies covering five pages, including me. I had seen her only once. Also on the list were the Governor, Attorney General, Mayor, two Senators, the Director of the American Psychological Association, Channel 6 TV, many doctors, and the local K-Mart.

Most paranoids are prolific writers and go on interminably in a *Highly Dramatic Style*. I did receive one letter, though, addressed to "Dr. *Ben* Wendorf" (???) and rubber-stamped all over with "confidential" and "personal mail." In it were two pages of Bible quotes and another page of chapter and verse citations. Judging from the passages cited, it appeared I (or at least Ben) was being accused of having an affair, apparently with my own sister! I categorically deny it, and so does Sis. There were no threats, no direct statements, and no signature. There was no follow-up. I have absolutely no idea who might have sent it or why they addressed me as "Ben," but the writer would certainly have to be someone pretty weird.

Projection is a difficult concept for some people to grasp and for many to accept. How can my own thoughts and feelings appear to me to be coming from you? Yet it is a common defense mechanism, a way of protecting oneself from desires, emotions, or ideas one finds unacceptable. It occurs frequently in marital relationships, where it may be complicated by the other spouse accepting the projection, identifying with it and even acting it out, so that it comes to be true. For example, a wife might feel stupid, incompetent, and inferior but deny to herself that she feels this way, because it makes her feel sad and anxious. Instead she perceives her husband to be critical, condescending, or insulting to her, taking offense at his every casual remark. The husband may become annoyed with his wife's defensiveness, begin to actually feel critical of her, and in fact to start pointing out how ridiculously she is behaving—i.e., to begin criticizing her. Her self-criticism has been denied and projected onto the husband. He then identifies with the projection and acts it out. This kind of interaction, called "projective identification," is one reason marriage counseling is so difficult. It's often nearly impossible to tell who is feeling what, whether one spouse is over-reacting to the other, or who started a cycle of projected interactions.

The most commonly projected feeling is probably anger, as in the classic "they're out to get me" paranoid. But hostility is not the only emotion subject to this mechanism. Lust is also a common example. A hospital patient once confided in me that a female patient was sexually attracted to him and had really been coming on to him in vocational therapy class. This surprised me, because the guy was kind of creepy, not to mention unattractive. He certainly was no match for this bright, classy, well-done-up young lady, who I also knew to have a very devoted fiance. Checking with the nursing staff, who always have the inside scoop on such matters, I found that the male patient had in fact been making a thorough nuisance of himself, blatantly propositioning not only this woman, but other female patients as well. His chart indicated that the man had a history of sexual misconduct going back to his childhood, when he himself had been molested. He'd also been severely punished for masturbating. This presumably explained his internal conflicts about sexuality, which led him to project his own desires onto others.

The mother of another former patient came in to complain about the man who has allegedly been stalking her for years. He follows her around, thinly disguising himself with different vehicles, wigs, false beards, and so on. He was supposedly interested in both her body and her money. She, too, had an elevated sense of her own attractiveness, and I didn't have the heart to tell her. But I did point out that she was bankrupt and unemployed. She maintained he was aiming at the proceeds from her best-selling book, a book she had yet to begin writing! She obviously had no idea how hard it is to make any money as an author, but she's an interesting example of one paranoid projecting both hostility and lust at the same time. This is a woman who has been victimized all her life, by her father, by two abusive husbands, by the world in general. She's one angry lady. She's also in love with her stalker, by her own admission. In fact, she's shown me several love letters she's written him and admits to many phone calls, even to going by his house. He's never written her back, and he's twice left town to get away from her, yet in her mind he's stalking her! She also admitted she's had numerous affairs herself, including a menage a trois with a man she'd never met before. She even admitted to a brief fling with the family pooch! Yet she believed her "stalker" is a sexual addict and she's not.

For anyone still doubtful about projection, my psychoanalytic buddy Dr. Paul Weir relates a bizarre experience that should be convincing. As he was driving home one night on a local freeway, he noticed another car rapidly approaching him from the rear, driving rather erratically and with no lights on. The car roared up, nearly rear-ending him, but then drifted back to a safe distance. This pattern was repeated several times, which Paul found distressing, even though the other driver seemed more distracted than threatening or aggressive. Exiting the interstate, Paul looked back to see the other vehicle still on his tail. He took a left at the first light, then quickly right and right again, the shadow sedan still glued to his bumper. The next left put him on his own street, but he didn't dare pull into his own driveway with this strange man right behind. So he drove on, zigzagging randomly through the streets of Homewood. The guy stayed right with him, now clearly following him, though making no attempt to contact him, shoot him, or run him off the road. Growing increasingly alarmed, Paul got the Homewood Police on his cell phone, reported what was going on, and told them he was coming in. Amazingly, when he turned into the parking lot of the Police Station, his mystery trailer pulled in right beside him—and rolled down his window to converse! Feeling a little safer in his current location, Dr. Weir cracked his own window, to hear the man out.

"Excuse me, friend," said the other driver. "You seemed to be having trouble controlling your vehicle, and I wondered if you were intoxicated. I thought you might need me to give you a ride home."

Paul said the man was so drunk he could barely hold his head up. Yet he had projected his own inebriated condition onto another driver, perceiving in him what he could evidently not accept in himself. Now that's projection!

One of the strangest people I ever worked with was also one of the first, a flabby, slightly effeminate sixteen-year-old named Kevin. Kevin was inattentive, impulsive, and hyperactive, yet also quite lazy. He loved money and he loved attention, and he would do *anything* to get either, so long as it didn't involve actual work. On field trips Kevin would dive under every Coke or candy machine to grope for dropped coins, and he had to be forcibly prevented from begging. He'd been referred to the PACE program by his school, where he'd been spotted fishing coins out of urinals with his tongue. Boys had peed on the coins. Kevin was exceptionally bright, but he was also gleefully, aggressively weird.

I got Kevin my second year at PACE and continued to see him occasionally after my internship ended. I got him because he was so obnoxious and resistant to therapy that no one else would take him, and the internship director gave me no choice. One of the first things I discovered about Kevin was that you couldn't walk down the corridor with him. He walked in a bouncy, loose-jointed fashion reminiscent of what the hippies called "truckin'," meandering all over the hall, literally caroming from wall to wall. Anyone walking abreast got bumped repeatedly, despite dedicated efforts to fend him off or to tack when he did. If you walked behind him he slowed to a near-crawl and if you walked ahead he wandered off on a money-hunting detour. He wouldn't run at all, though another staff member and I succeeded in prodding him into a fairly rapid shuffle by trotting along and popping his butt with a ping-pong paddle. We gave it up as a hopeless cause when it became apparent that Kevin *liked* being swatted. The ethicality of paddling him was questionable enough, even in those primitive times, but involving ourselves in a sado-masochistic menage a trois was just too kinky for my colleague and me.

Kevin had another odd habit while walking: whenever he passed by another adolescent, he flinched, as if in fear of being hit. Granted, his annoying habits and dubious sexuality had elicited a considerable amount of abuse from his peers, but Kevin flinched away from even the littlest and most timid. Besides, nobody was going to hit him with a staff member in attendance, since any aggression earned twenty minutes in the cooler. It was a surprisingly offensive and maddening habit, which just made one want to beat the stuffing out of him.

It wasn't hard to relate to Kevin intellectually, as he was bright and curious and loved to talk, especially about his own bizarre behavior. My first real therapeutic intervention, however, was to suggest he raise his price for performing fellatio. Kevin thought of himself as homosexual at that time, though he really wasn't sexually motivated much at all. He thought giving blow jobs was a sure-fire way to garner both abusive attention and a little money, his two primary motivators, simultaneously. "Kevin," I told him, "those boys are ripping you off; at 25 cents a pop they're not your true friends. You can easily charge fifteen, even twenty dollars for a first-class blow-job."

That really captured Kevin's attention. Not only had I not been grossed out or critical of him—which is of course what he wanted— I'd raised his income eighty times over. Suddenly I was a guy worth listening to, even if I was still to be the target of his endless con artistry. And it wasn't as totally inappropriate as it might sound. I'd given Kevin a little bit of a reality check while showing him some acceptance of his eccentric ways. I'd shown that I was concerned with his welfare and gotten him to begin looking after his own best interests instead of pandering to others and being abused in return. By implicitly encouraging an inappropriate behavior, I'd taken away both its shock value and its utility as an act of rebellion. Then I asked if his friends ever gave *him* a blow-job, knowing of course that they did not. "Some friends," I snorted. That really got him thinking, and it wasn't long before he decided he had a little too much self-respect to remain in the fellatio business.

His one exception to this rule was Walker, the mute boy with whom Kevin had a unique and in some ways genuine relationship. For reasons we were never able to discover, Walker refused to talk. He'd rarely answer, and then only in an inaudible whisper, but mostly he remained totally silent. We knew he *could* talk, as he carried on lengthy discussions with Kevin, but our best efforts to produce speech were miserably ineffective. Placed in the cooler with the door unlocked, Walker would sit for hours rather than ask to be let out, which was all we required for his release. Before my time at PACE someone had told Walker he could have a meal only when he asked for it loudly enough to be heard six feet away. Walker lost ten pounds before that therapeutic venture was abandoned. We finally sent Walker home, still as silent as a lamppost. Meanwhile, he and Kevin maintained a close relationship, which centered on long conversations in the shower and, apparently, mutual fellatio. This was Kevin's only free sex at that time and the only mutual sexual relationship he had experienced. Though bizarre and inappropriate, the relationship was good for both of them, and we hated to discourage it.

Kevin used even his intelligence to be eccentric and annoying. His first questions for me were "what is your birth date?" and "what kind of car do you drive?" When I told him, he informed me that the wheelbase of my 1959 Chevy BelAir was 127.4 inches (or whatever it was). Understandably skeptical, I dug out the owner's manual and checked; he was dead on, to the tenth of an inch. It turned out Kevin knew the wheelbase of every car ever manufactured in America, knowledge he insisted on sharing at the least provocation. He also knew the birth date of everyone he'd ever met. He could not explain these peculiar interests to my satisfaction, but I had to be impressed with his prodigious memory. Three years later he revealed that he also "did" clothing and he described exactly the shirt I'd been wearing the first time he saw me.

The PACE program was a very strictly run "token economy." Each patient had a specific set of behaviors for which he earned points or "tokens" on a daily basis. A clean room was worth two points; completing schoolwork was worth ten; speaking in group therapy was good for one to five, depending on the individual's program. Tokens were good motivators because they were used to purchase both luxuries and necessities on the unit. Supper cost five tokens, cigarettes one token, a home visit twenty tokens. We received a daily print-out on each patient and could fine-tune their programs as needed. It was a good therapy program and it gave the staff a great deal of control over patient behavior, which was what we were supposed to change.

Except for Kevin. Kevin managed to subvert the system in the interest of maintaining his "craziness," continuing to misbehave and act out, yet still earning almost all his tokens. One of his best ploys was to sabotage our programs with reverse psychology, deciding he liked our punishments and didn't want our rewards. Most of the kids would roll naked over broken glass to make a home visit. Kevin decided he liked PACE better and quit going home at all, driving the weekend staff half crazy and saving twenty tokens at the same time. Most of the kids hated sleeping in the hallway, which you did if you hadn't earned and purchased a room for the night. Kevin liked it because he could stay awake all night and bug the graveyard nursing shift. Besides, nobody could beat him up in the hall. If he really did want a reward he'd amassed and hoarded such a huge "bank account" he always had sufficient tokens to buy it. One of my most effective therapeutic interventions was to freeze Kevin's account. Suddenly he went from a token millionaire to a veritable pauper who had to start earning points again. He hated it, resented me, and thought me terribly unfair, which was true enough. But he also realized that ultimately my position of responsibility gave me more power than his position of irresponsibility. He decided he wanted to change, to be "normal," and to graduate and go home. He asked me for help.

I did help, but it wasn't easy. Kevin was so engrained in trying to act weird and had such a knack for it, that he seemed odd even when he attempted normal behavior. We tried to get him a part-time job, but he couldn't resist asking fellow employees about their wheelbases. I tried to teach him how to drive, foolishly volunteering my own vehicle (which by now was a Volkswagen, wheelbase—well, never mind). Kevin drove like he walked down hallways, paying no attention to the task at hand, chattering on endlessly, and using lanes, shoulders, and lawns indiscriminately. He might have been a sailor on a hard upwind course, tacking back and forth, spreading chaos before him. I quickly gave up while my shock absorbers and coronary arteries were still functional. We finally just graduated Kevin and sent him home, knowing he and his family could not tolerate each other more than a few days. It seemed we had failed Kevin almost completely.

Oddly, Kevin took matters under his own advisement and ended up doing fairly well, in his own peculiar fashion. He let his hair grow and dressed as a hippie. It was all he could afford, and, besides, his eccentricities fit smoothly and acceptably into the hippie subculture of the early '70s. He scrounged up a dilapidated panel truck, a vehicle so utterly trashed that people made way for him, knowing he had nothing to lose in a wreck. He used it to scour the roadways, scavenging junk furniture he could sell cheap to other hippies, winos, and graduate students. He even managed to remedy his sexual kinks while hitching across the country from one hippie crash pad to another. "Bob," he proudly announced on one of his occasional social calls, "I'm straight." He'd ended up on a cold night sharing a sleeping bag with a warm and friendly young girl. She'd accomplished in an evening what two years of inpatient psychotherapy hadn't even touched. I admired her expertise and was happy for both of them.

In many ways Kevin resembled the Asperger's patients I was to see over twenty years later, but at that time Asperger's was unknown in this country. He was physically clumsy, socially inept, bright but impulsive and unfocused. He was obsessively preoccupied with a very narrow and rather bizarre set of interests (wheelbases and birth dates). What set Kevin apart was the cleverness of his con artistry and the gleefulness of his eccentricities. It doesn't give Kevin full credit to call him "merely" weird.

The diagnosis of weirdness is inevitably a subjective one. One person's eccentricity is another's creativity. What is considered weird varies from one era to another, and from society to society, just as psychosis does. Kevin was just another ordinary "freak" to his hippie friends, while a man in a Brooks Brothers suit would seem pretty odd in a commune or crash pad. It's no longer weird to practice Chinese herbal medicine, to consider oneself a "witch," or to believe in "channeling" with dead spirits. Well, at least not *as* weird. Weirdness makes people interesting, and some of the weirdest people are also the most creative and original. It's not my job to change people's weirdness unless they want to change or they're hurting somebody. Meanwhile, my patients are sometimes afraid of shocking me with their weird habits. After treating thousands of hyperactive kids, rebellious adolescents, and depressed adults, my response to them is to "bring it on." I don't shock easily anymore, and I'm always delighted to hear of a new way to be weird.

CHAPTER TEN
Elvis and Asperger's

THE HIGHLIGHT OF MY FIFTIETH BIRTHDAY, and one of the most touching moments of my career, was to be serenaded by Elvis Presley. In full rhinestone-studded leather jump suit and shades, the King of Rock and Roll sang "Happy Birthday" to me in my office. It wasn't actually Elvis, of course, but in some ways this impersonator was more remarkable than the real owner of Graceland. For this Elvis was my long-time and presumably permanent patient Donald, and Donald suffers from a little-known psychiatric condition called Asperger's Disorder. His story is a tale of tragedy and triumph, of a man who has struggled with life and himself and his illness at great cost, but with considerable success.

When I first met Donald I didn't know he had Asperger's, but then neither did he, nor his psychiatrist. I'd never heard of Asperger's, and neither had they. Since then I've seen a number of Asperger's patients and realized a couple of old ones also suffered from this syndrome. Donald was severely depressed and had a history of attempted suicide, which had several times landed him in psychiatric hospitals. He was obsessive-compulsive and as anxious as anyone I've ever seen, especially in social situations. He also was easily over-loaded by excessive stimulation, especially noise, and would go into either a panic attack or a sudden episode of rage. He couldn't drive most places alone and couldn't handle the freeways at all. With high speeds and multiple lanes there was simply too much happening for him to deal with it all, and he was terrified of having an accident and hurting someone. (Dustin Hoffman's character in the movie *Rain Man* also had Asperger's, I believe, and also feared the Interstates, forcing Tom Cruise's character to take secondary roads.) Donald worried almost paranoically over comments he'd made years ago, which someone might have found offensive and might yet beat him up about. Donald had been diagnosed with major depression, obsessive-compulsive disorder, bipolar disorder, paranoid schizophrenia, attention deficit hyperactivity disorder, social phobia, panic disorder, and a raft of other illnesses, but he really didn't fit the classical picture for any of them. He'd been on anti-psychotics, anti-depressants, and anti-anxiety medications, and we even tried him briefly on Ritalin (for ADHD). When I met him he was still employed, but barely hanging on. To complicate matters even further, Donald also suffered from a form of chronic colitis or irritable bowel syndrome closely resembling Crohn's Disease. He was subject to bouts of sudden, explosive, and bloody diarrhea, which struck without warning and left him weakened and, often, embarrassed. His illness was exacerbated by stress, and Donald had plenty of that.

Donald was looking for help with stress management, assertiveness training, low self-esteem, and relationship problems. His psychiatrist had put him on medical leave, because he'd gotten so stressed he'd stomped off the line at work, ranting about "kicking someone's ass." Ordinarily he's the mildest, gentlest, most tender-hearted people-pleaser you ever met, but when he gets rattled Donald can curse like a modern comedian. His potential for violence, however, is about the same as a pudding-pop. Nonetheless, we began working on how to handle work stress, how to deal with perceived injustices assertively and without verbal violence. We worked on dealing more effectively with his co-workers and his parents, as he had essentially no other relationships, although he had actually dated some in the past. I found him to be an eager student but a rather slow learner. Somehow, Donald just seemed to process information differently.

In fact, as I got to know Donald better, I found him increasingly puzzling. He was employed in a laborer's job, yet he was exceptionally well-read and had completed two years of college—after dropping out of high school and obtaining a G.E.D. He was logical and articulate, yet his conversation had an odd, wooden quality to it. Even when joking there was little inflection in his speech, and he made very little eye contact. Intensely eager for others' approval, he had no real friends, and, at thirty-six, was back living with his parents. A skinny, uncoordinated kid who could scarcely run, he'd majored for a time in physical education and was fascinated with weight-lifting and muscle-builders. Diagnostically, Donald was an enigma, so I gave him an MMPI, the number one personality test in psychology. It came back with startling results.

As expected, Donald's MMPI showed he was extremely anxious and depressed, with these scales literally pushing the top of the chart. He denied any hallucinations and did not seem delusional, yet indicators of psychosis were also extremely elevated, confirming there was something decidedly peculiar about his thought processes. The tendency to develop stress-related physical illnesses was evident in his profile, as was his poor impulse control, alternating with rigid over-control. Despite his nervous, hyperactive appearance, he did not look at all manic. The profile showed a lot of psychopathology, but its pattern made little sense and correlated only roughly with the clinical picture. Donald's case was looking curiouser and curiouser, until I happened upon a brief description of Asperger's Disorder in an unrelated professional article. As I sought out further literature, I realized the diagnostic criteria fit Donald beautifully. Now we were finally getting somewhere.

Asperger's Disorder is a high-functioning variant of Autism, which some research suggests is inherited genetically and is genetically linked to Bipolar Disorder (manic-depressive illness) but not to classical autism or to schizophrenia. This fit with Donald, whose father, while marrying, raising two children, and successfully working, has no really close friends except a hound dog, has difficulty conversing, and presents a slightly eccentric appearance. Donald's brother has Bipolar Disorder. Another Asperger's patient, the Professor described below, has a son who can only be described as odd, immature, and "goofy," clearly also an Asperger's sufferer. I don't want to over-state the genetic case, however. As with most major psychiatric and many physical illnesses, Asperger's Disorder may require both an underlying genetic predisposition and some sort of environmental trigger. This may be a viral infection or perhaps some sort of trauma, as is often seen in schizophrenia. Another Asperger's patient, for example, does have a father with mildly autistic tendencies. But he was progressing pretty normally until he was severely sexually abused as a toddler. His behavior not only regressed, but took on a strongly autistic flavor. Asperger's has been classified as a pervasive developmental disorder, akin to, but involving a higher level of intellectual and social functioning than, autism. The two disorders are similar but have significant differences. Technically, as of the recent publication of the *Diagnostic and Statistical Manual* (Edition V) of the American Psychiatric Association, Asperger's now exists as a separate diagnosis, but is simply listed as an Autistic Spectrum Disorder, that is, on the same spectrum as classical (Kanner's) autism. I have chosen to stick with the term "Asperger's" because I disagree strongly with the DSM-V revised diagnostic criteria and classification. So do many other psychologists and psychiatrists. I believe the two, while similar in some ways, are distinctly different and probably have different genetics. Autistic patients typically score in the retarded range on IQ tests, while Asperger's patients often score in ranges considered normal. The genetics look different. Most importantly, most autistics have little or no interest in human relationships, while, in many instances, Asperger's desperately want to have and sustain them.

The classically autistic person is literally caught in his own little world and has essentially no, or at best minimal, relationships with others. Many do not speak or do so in such a manner as to be unintelligible. Often they simply echo the words of others. They do not seem to recognize people as essentially different from other objects in the world, and many refuse to be hugged or kissed. They may react strangely to various stimuli or engage in nearly constant manneristic behavior. For example, I worked with one autistic child who loved to bang pots and pans as loudly as possible, yet screamed as if in agony at a Brahms Symphony. Another spent all day spinning every moveable object between the palms of his hands.

In contrast, the Asperger's patient has normal speech, except that inflection seems lacking, and nonverbal communication generally is poor. My "Professor" spoke always in a monotone, and one could never tell from his facial expression if he was elated or enraged. His son spoke in a high-pitched, almost sing-song voice. While the classical autistic person has no social interest, the Asperger's patient desperately desires relationships, but, sadly, finds it extremely difficult to relate effectively with others. Their social skills are lacking; they communicate oddly; they have poor emotional control; and their interests are so narrow and often so eccentric, that they just seem out of phase interpersonally. Raymond, the patient so brilliantly portrayed by Dustin Hoffman in the movie *Rain Man,* was probably suffering from Asperger's Disorder, although he also displayed many more classically autistic traits. Notice the flat, wooden quality to his speech, as well as his lack of eye contact, severely limited social skills, and odd preoccupation with numbers and certain TV shows. Notice the sudden rage or panic reactions and the poor physical coordination, characteristics also shared with Donald and the abused young man described above. Notice also that he did form a kind of limited but real relationship with his brother, sensitively played by Tom Cruise. In his early forties, Donald is living at home again and his best friends are his mom—and me. He has dated briefly in the past and has formed casual friendships with the owner of a T-shirt shop, a "personal trainer," and former co-workers. He has no really close friendships. Still, his ability to relate as well as he does is a remarkable achievement. Indeed, except for his rare cussing fits, Donald is a kind gentleman with a good sense of humor. I am proud to call him my friend.

My "Professor" was also a decent, caring, and responsible person, yet had tremendous interpersonal and career difficulties. He came in with his wife, also a teacher, who was on the verge of divorcing him because she needed "a husband, not another child." The Professor held a doctorate in biochemistry and was extremely well-versed in his field. Yet he was teaching at a junior college because he couldn't seem to write up his research in a way acceptable to the journals and had been denied tenure at the state university. Further, other faculty and staff complained that he was rude to them, and students were tired of hounding him to get their papers graded, so even this lower-level job was endangered. He loved his kids and played well with them, but he disciplined either too harshly or not at all, sometimes involved them in dangerous play, and often simply forgot he was babysitting and wandered off to do his own thing. His wife couldn't trust him alone with the kids and had to hire sitters when he was available for free! He had trouble relating sexually as well, preferring masturbation with his wife's underwear as a fetishistic object to actually making love to the real thing. She finally got so frustrated she had an affair, and when that wasn't enough she divorced him. The Professor quickly found himself an asexual woman who loved mothering him, and who both dominated and took care of him faithfully. He wasn't a bad guy, just one too self-absorbed to relate to others. His judgment was a bit off, too, as in his hobby of playing with explosives in his back yard.

Both classical autistics and Asperger's patients tend to develop obsessive preoccupations, but of a very different quality. The autistic patient is likely to focus on objects or repeated manneristic behaviors, such as the boy who liked pots and pans or my constant "spinner." The Asperger's patient as a child may play in a stereotyped manner with a few toys, such as lining up a collection of toy trucks over and over again. As an adult he is more likely to be obsessed in an anxious, worrisome way, or simply to have a very constricted set of interests. Donald is much too anxious to drive at night, to go new places, or to take the Interstates, or to drive at all if there is *any* chance of rain. He still frets over imagined disputes from two decades ago. More to the point, he is utterly absorbed in muscle magazines and Elvis. He knows his interests are narrow and obsessive, not shared by others, even a bit silly, since his physical problems prevent him from weight-lifting himself. He's actually a bit embarrassed by the Elvis fixation, as he sees it (unfairly, I think) as a "redneck" attraction unbecoming to a well-educated person such as himself. Yet he regales me with Elvis trivia and brings me souvenirs from his trips to Graceland. I love my "shades" and handkerchief. He also seems to assume that I may have a similar preoccupation, though he's aware I'm not a super Elvis fan. (I like Elvis; I'm just not obsessed.) Finding that I like the Beatles, he's bought me several books and five very attractive Beatles T-shirts. But again, while I *like* the Beatles, they're not necessarily my very favorite band. I'm not complaining, though, as the gifts are lovely and thoughtful. Besides, where do you buy a shirt with Arturo Sandoval, Pat Metheny, or Strunz and Farah on it?

The Professor had his quirky preoccupations too, although they varied more than Donald's. For a while he made exact replicas of Native American tools and weapons, even demonstrating the manufacturing art at local elementary schools. He progressed to carving perfect geometric solids out of limestone, a rather unforgiving medium and an arcane pastime of dubious value. His wife left him when he became preoccupied with "experimenting" with plastic explosives. A friend of mine reports that her brother, another Asperger's patient, collects maps and redraws them beautifully in exquisite detail.

Both autism and Asperger's appear to be congenital and probably genetic. Both tend to involve hyperactivity, though neither typically responds well to stimulants such as Ritalin or Adderall. Both often include motoric clumsiness or incoordination, although the Professor's fine and gross-motor coordination were exceptionally good. Autistic persons are difficult to test, especially verbally, and usually score in the mentally retarded range. Asperger's patients typically score as having average intelligence or better. Both tend to have obsessive preoccupations such as Indian tool-making, Elvis, or Judge Wapner's TV court. And both can possess extraordinary talents in specific areas, such as the Professor's carving skills or Rain Man's phenomenal memory for numbers.

We don't know just what's going on in the brains of persons with Asperger's or other forms of autism. Their unusual ways of communicating suggest a partial answer: maybe they simply tend to process verbal and nonverbal information in unusual ways. This was my initial observation about Donald and what led me to research Asperger's in the first place. Uta Frith, in her book on *Autism and Asperger Syndrome*, provides another example suggesting such a processing problem. She discusses the autobiography of Dr. Temple Grandin, entitled *Emergence: Labeled Autistic*. Dr. Grandin has a Ph.D. in animal science, runs her own consulting company, designs livestock facilities and has over two hundred professional publications. Yet she clearly suffers from Asperger's Disorder, a fact which may be discerned even from her writing. As Dr. Frith points out, Dr. Grandin's work betrays a limited ability to relate to others, a lack of empathy or emotional awareness (except for animals), and a perseverative preoccupation with the bizarre "squeeze machine" she created to replicate the experience of being hugged—an experience she found intolerable with real people. Featured in a *Nature* program on the mind, Dr. Grandin described herself as a radically visual thinker. Her thoughts come not in words, but in pictures, which she believes is helpful to her in designing livestock corrals, ramps, and so on. Similarly, in *Rain Man* the Asperger's number genius explains to his brother that he mentally *sees* the numbers he memorizes. How generally true her observations may be, Dr. Grandin at least demonstrates convincingly that some Asperger's sufferers, though eccentric, may be highly intelligent. My other young autistic, now adolescent, is quite bright and excels in everything but spelling and reading. And he can't take lecture notes, though he remembers most of the lecture anyway. When I talked with him about information processing and visual thinking, he said that is *exactly* how it is with him. "I see my thoughts as pictures," he explained.

Another of my Asperger's patients provides in her writing a glimpse of the idiosyncratic word-processing that characterizes her own thinking. The following is excerpted from a high school term paper on current events, specifically the raising of a new, non-Confederate flag for the State of Georgia: "This article is about a Georgia flag raised at the Capitol. Who is talking Brooks, and what Georgia's Capitol Dome, and why because Georgia has a new flag, and the how is Georgia gets a new flag to represent the State by winning the crown. This article is also about how Georgia's flag is raised by the white figure Miss Freedom, and and (*sic*) on Wednesday, the flag is raised on a cloudy day."

Referring to the original newspaper article, it is clear that this patient has understood the adoption and raising of a new flag. But she has taken the statue of Miss Freedom to be a real person and not understood the symbolic importance of the cloudless day (which, indeed, she misquotes as cloudy). Further, while she has clearly understood the assignment accurately, she has incorporated its instructions into the paper itself, failing to distinguish between them and the material to be reported. Obviously she was told to include the "what, where, when, why, who, and how" of the article, and so she did! Thus, her logic is not wrong, just idiosyncratic. She fails to distinguish between content and process, just as Asperger's patients typically have difficulty with the nonverbal, or process, level of spoken communication.

More broadly, the idea of Asperger's as a different manner of processing information leads us to speculate about other people who "think differently." Certainly we know that people think, or process information, in ways that are different but nonetheless quite valid or correct. Some people think in logical, verbal terms, while others grasp the world intuitively or via sensory input. This is the basis for the Myers-Briggs Type Inventory, a psychological test which classifies people according to their preferred modes of perceiving the world. I think of my old buddy Bobby DeBourbon, a strongly visual and highly intuitive thinker. Bobby and I would see the same patient and come up with the same treatment plan, but I did it by logical analysis of the patient's behavior, while Bobby simply "knew" this course of action felt right. We fished every weekend at the same lake in central Illinois. I could have provided either detailed verbal instructions on how to get there or drawn an accurate map. Bobby could do neither, yet he always got there—by "intuition." Some psychologists and educators see dyslexics, even possibly autistics, not as "disordered" but as differently ordered, "gifted," and possessed of a potentially valuable and creative way of perceiving and analyzing reality. Are we inadvertently suppressing valuable, even unique perspectives by trying to "normalize" their styles of thought? Isn't creativity exactly the process of seeing reality in a new way? Einstein was a visual thinker, like Dr. Grandin, and very probably dyslexic. There is even considerable evidence to suggest he may have suffered—if that's the word—from Asperger's. Edison was certainly dyslexic, and Leonardo DaVinci may also have been. Many dyslexic and autistic individuals are amazingly creative and gifted in specific ways. Is the neurologically funny wiring that makes them dyslexic also what makes them creative? Should they be treated or simply appreciated?

There is no cure for Asperger's Disorder. Treatment is supportive and focused on relief of specific symptoms. I've helped Donald drive a bit more, got him working out a bit, smoothed out his family relationships, and boosted his self-esteem. He's a little less anxious and not depressed or suicidal. But he's still not quite right. He's still basically Donald, which he and I have decided is okay. As much as anything, I've helped him to understand his condition and himself, so that his problem has a name, and he doesn't blame himself for his failings or faults. I'm glad I could help; he's certainly enriched my life, and I hope I've done the same for him.

Psychotherapy is intended to be a time-limited process, which ends when problems are resolved. But what of a patient, like Donald, whose problems (if such they be) will never be fully resolved? Therapists are taught not to take their patients home with them (either literally or figuratively), but sometimes you can't really help it. I've been seeing Donald every couple of months for years, and he's so sweet and thoughtful, and so funny with my staff (with some assistance from his mom) that he became a favorite of the whole office. He was part of our office family, and I'm part of his, and I continue to be long even after my retirement from active practice. I'm okay with that. Besides, he and his family have been wonderfully supportive of me through some family medical crises. He sent me a lovely card, and his father made my son a cane which provided for months his only mode of ambulation. I referred him to my brother for therapy, and he and I meet for lunch occasionally. I put on a Beatles shirt, and Donald wears his "Blue Hawaii" shirt, and we go for barbeque. As Elvis would say, we're "taking care of business."

CHAPTER 11

Narcissus and Echo

ATHLETICALLY BUILT AND RUGGEDLY handsome, Augustus could have been the Roman emperor for whom he was named. He wasn't the sort of man you'd call "Augie" or "Gus" for short. He was an extremely competitive golfer, was always dressed in casual, fashionable, and expensive golf clothes, and carried himself with an air of nobility. He was quite vain. His wife Gloria was an even more striking figure, tall and statuesque, despite having borne several children. Her clothes were dramatic but tasteful and becoming. Her silver hair was cropped shockingly short, as if to emphasize the high cheekbones and full lips of the successful model she'd been. She was articulate and theatrical. She was glorious. Together Augustus and Gloria were a couple from a Greek myth, a pair to live on in legend and song. Their marriage was like two stars colliding in a supernovic explosion, spewing vast amounts of energy and star-stuff, that is, a typical Borderline/ Narcissist relationship.

I can't think of Gloria and Augustus without getting all mythic, as their relationship was reminiscent of at least two couples from Greek mythology. Augustus was ten years older than Gloria and had had the good fortune to be "adopted" by a wealthy old homosexual business- man named Eddie Pusch. Thus, he was living the life of a rich playboy, despite his own lack of career accomplishment, spending more time on the golf course than at the office. The exact nature of his relationship with his mentor and benefactor, who also consulted me about their marriage, was unclear. Gloria and I assumed it included sexual favors, but Augustus furiously denied it. Gloria was a poor but beautiful country girl who had been married briefly to an abusive and psychotic small-town politico in. She'd originally been named "Tiffany Glass," after a catalogue ad for a reproduction lamp. Augustus took her under his wing and began to recreate her in his own image, just as Pygmalion sculpted Galatea into the perfect woman. He renamed her "Gloria Monday," evidently thinking of the Stones' song "Ruby Tuesday." He transformed and reinvented her. It was a kind of a sick transit from Tiffany Glass to Gloria Monday, and Augustus was the conductor.

He did pretty well at it, too, launching her on a successful modeling career, helping her through college, and eventually landing her a job as a financial counselor. They also produced some gorgeous children. Augustus was Gloria's mentor, father-confessor, charm school teacher, critic, and lover. He took her from a rough chunk of field stone to a Carrera marble statue, replacing her cotton shifts with silk pant suits and her rural East Texas twang with a polished and cosmopolitan diction. She was a piece of work, and he was rightly proud of his accomplishment. "Glo" was grateful and adored him. At first. But, just like Pygmalion, who sculpted Galatea because of his underlying hostility to women, then found himself in love with a stone image, Augustus eventually found himself married to a woman whose heart was cold to him.

Unfortunately, Gloria and Augustus also resembled another mythic couple, Narcissus and Echo. Narcissus, you'll recall, was so amazingly handsome that anyone who saw his face would immediately fall in love with him. Narcissus was so beautiful they named a flower for him, but like Pygmalion, he was basically hostile to women and scorned their love for him, preferring his own self-absorption. Narcissus happened to see his own face reflected in a pool of water and promptly fell in love with his own image. So caught up in self-adoration was he that Narcissus never heard Echo, a beautiful nymph, when she spoke to him of her own love. And all she got back from him was the echo of her own voice. Augustus had a Narcissistic personality disorder of highly malignant proportions. Glo got to play the part of Echo, adoring a man who adored only himself.

Narcissism is a psychological defense mechanism which can come to dominate and distort one's entire personality. We all need to shield our egos from threats to our self-esteem. We rationalize our failures, deny our faults, or project blame onto others. These maneuvers constitute a minor distortion of reality, but they enable us to keep our egos intact when they are faced with unpleasant truths about ourselves. But the Narcissist carries this defensive move to extremes. Narcissists start life well enough, receiving love and nurturing from their mothers. Basking in the radiant glow of an adoring mom, they experience themselves as "special," as loveable and capable individuals. But somewhere in early childhood they also have an experience of being unloveable, inadequate, inferior, or incompetent. Perhaps they suffer from a handicap or physical infirmity, or maybe they are disfigured, or maybe they're just seen as ugly. Perhaps they are ridiculed by their classmates for living on the wrong side of the tracks and dressing in old tattered hand-me-downs. For some narcissists it was simply too much of a rejection for their parents to have another child and then to give the new baby all the love and attention formerly reserved for them. ("What, I wasn't good enough, so you had to have another kid?") Whatever it is, something happens to indicate to the young narcissist that he just isn't good enough. Far from being "special," he is in fact fundamentally inadequate and inferior.

This "narcissistic injury" is experienced as a profound insult to the newly formed young ego. It stamps him with a self-image that is simply intolerable and provides no basis for self-esteem. He yearns to return to his old symbiotic bond with his mother and to experience himself again as "The Special One." So he turns to the defensive maneuver called narcissism. Life has provided him with two contradictory sets of experiences about himself. In one he is defined as inferior, inadequate, and unloveable. In the other he is superior, adorable, and special. It's an easy choice. He decides that in fact he is not inferior; on the contrary, he is *better* than all the others. Oh, they don't understand and appreciate him, but if they only knew how wonderful he was, they would flock to be near him and shower him with praise and affection. The narcissist creates for himself (I use the masculine pronoun because pathological narcissism in our society is more common in men, although it is unclear whether this represents a true, underlying gender difference or merely a societal stereotype) a new self-image, which he erects in grandiose terms. Then he sets out to prove to all the world how truly superior he is—so that he'll be able to believe it himself and recapture the feeling of being "special."

In so doing, however, the narcissist strays from the path of reality. What he has created is a grandiose but *false* self, which he then "falls in love" with. He does not possess true self-love or self-esteem, but only infatuation with a false *image* of himself. While he displays an incredible arrogance and cockiness, he lacks genuine self-confidence. Narcissists demand special privileges and attention because they feel entitled to it, by virtue of their superiority. They should not have to stand in line like the common folk, should never be caught in traffic, should always have the best table in the house and be served first. Yet they are never at peace with themselves and bounce back and forth between feelings of superiority and feelings of inferiority. Internally they are at war with themselves, and they constantly fear being unmasked, revealing the inadequate child within them. Even if they can really become as superior and grand as they pretend to be, they are never quite comfortable with themselves, because they know it's all an image, a facade, a sham. And anything that tarnishes the all-important image, questions the grandiosity, or implies any criticism is experienced as a repeat of the original narcissistic injury—and throws the narcissist into a rage. It is sometimes even a violent rage.

Narcissists are emotionally fixated at the age the game began— say three to five years of age. That's why they fly into rages, the emotional reaction of a child, not an adult. It's also why they have a boyish charm about them that is highly enticing to many females. And it's why there's also a hurt-little-boy quality about them which draws women to mother them. Unfortunately, lacking true self-love, the narcissist is incapable of loving others either. Narcissists are too self-absorbed to be considerate of others. They are too insecure to trust in the other's love, and their defense mechanisms keep people from getting close to them. They are too perfect and grandiose to admit they need someone else, so they denigrate and devalue their mates. Remember the part in the myth that Echo plays? Just so, our Gloria was Echo to Augustus' Narcissus, the recipient of his outrageous and abusive tantrums, but not of his love and affection. And Gloria was also cold-hearted Galatea, who could not return the affection of her creator.

To be totally fair, I should note that I am presenting one view of the development of narcissism, one which holds true clinically and makes sense to me. But there are others. There is, for example, some reason to suspect that there may be genetic influences in at least some cases. Certainly the impulsivity and emotional reactivity of narcissists can be genetic. And it is well-recognized that narcissistic fathers tend to raise narcissistic sons. What we don't know for sure is whether the transmission is genetic or whether the sons become narcissistic because the fathers insult, denigrate, and demean them in an effort to bolster their own grandiose egos. Or both. Societal influences also need to be considered, especially since narcissism seems to be growing rapidly in our own society. Ours has been called "The Age of Narcissism," and certainly the disorder seems more prevalent everywhere from my office to the Oval Office. I've sure seen a lot more narcissists in my own practice, which I attributed at first either to over-diagnosis or to my own increased ability to spot them. Perhaps I'm just projecting my own narcissism onto my patients. But my friend Paul Weir reports the same thing in his practice. He tells me he's tired of getting chewed out for not being sympathetic enough when his patients' abused children refuse to see them again, their wives dump them for their philandering, or their money-grubbing mistresses aren't sufficiently fawning and attentive. Funny; Paul's always there for me. At a minimum, one would have to say that our society tolerates and even supports narcissism, if not actively promoting it. It is certainly a *me-first, look-good, get-all-you-can* culture. Note that the current craze is the "selfie," which is essentially a photo glorifying one's self, sent to anyone who'll look at it.

Augustus began his career in narcissism at the age of three, watching helplessly as his father severely beat his mother. Little Augustus was frightened, enraged, and humiliated to see his beloved mother assaulted, as he himself cowered in the corner. He felt utterly inadequate. He was angry at his father, although he later came to identify with him and to adopt his abusive style of relating to women. He was angry at his mother for allowing herself to be abused and for making him feel inadequate and ashamed. His disrespect for women, his sense of inability to meet their needs, and his frustration at not meeting his own self-esteem needs carried over into his every adult relationship with women, and especially with his wife. Like his father, Augustus despised, devalued, and desired women, and like his father he was manipulative, insulting, unfaithful, and assaultive to them. He screamed and raged at Gloria and repeatedly beat her with telephones, dishware, and his fists, often requiring medical care for the injuries he inflicted. If narcissism can range from a normal defense mechanist to outright sociopathy, Augustus was certainly pushing the antisocial end of the spectrum.

When I explained narcissism to him Augustus quietly sobbed like a small boy. He agreed completely with this diagnosis and was greatly relieved that someone understood his inner turmoil and terrible fear of inadequacy. He described himself as a shy, timid child, who preferred not to engage in the mandatory male activity for his family, namely hunting. For this he had been ridiculed, mocked, and humiliated by his cruel and domineering father. He was called a "sissy" and a "queer." At twelve he was told to shoot his own dog, and when he refused his father took the gun and killed the poor hound in front of Augustus. Augustus swore to become a "real man"—which meant a fierce competitor, a ruthless businessman, a commanding husband, and a success at any cost. In addition, he became a braggart, a con artist, and a bully. When his wife was sad or anxious he took it as a personal affront, a sign of his inadequacy to take care of her (as he'd failed to take care of his mother) and he hated her for it.

As one might guess, Gloria also came from a dysfunctional family and had her own personality problems. Her father was a gambler, philanderer, and alcoholic who beat young Gloria occasionally and her mother quite regularly. She needed a father's love in the worst way, having gotten precious little of it from her own dear Dad, and at seventeen she thought she'd found it in Augustus. He was twenty-seven and already drinking pretty heavily himself, but he looked like a Greek god, and he showered her with his blessings. He took her in and taught her the finer things in life. He made her his sex toy, and she would do whatever he wanted—sado-masochism, bondage, menages a trois, anything. Yet what he wanted was mostly to chase other women and to play with himself. By the time I met them, years later, Augustus was forty-six and was masturbating several times a day, often with Gloria watching his performance. He had intercourse infrequently and mostly with some other woman. True narcissism, after all, is autoerotic, a distorted form of self-love, and a relative inability to love others. Just as he loved not his true self, but only the grandiose false image of himself, Augustus did not love women for themselves. He loved only the *image* of women, the *appearance* of them, especially the naked and erotic images portrayed in his considerable collection of pornography. And he loved making them love and adore him.

Again, I'm using mostly men as examples of narcissistic self-absorption, but it certainly exists in women as well. For example, I treated a woman whose daughter found her collection of pornographic videos, most of which starred *herself* and a series of former lovers. She just loved to watch herself being adored by the men she used and tossed out with the trash. This wasn't about passion, eroticism, or love, just about distorted self-love—i.e., narcissism.

After a few years of their bizarre relationship, Glo had gotten tired of his cheating and abuse and had left Augustus for a psychotic but wealthy county official twenty years her senior. He kept her out of law school and mostly pregnant (two kids in four years) and often nursing cuts and bruises from *his* beatings. Eventually she resumed her affair with Augustus, got pregnant by him, and divorced her first husband to marry him. Augustus had finally won her, but he never forgave her for the insult of marrying another man.

When we marry we seek to regain the almost symbiotic bond we had as infants with our adoring mothers. We seek the perfect loving parent, and being "in love" we are crazy enough to believe we've found it. If we were lacking in parental love, we seek to find it. Having never known a father's love, Gloria was unconsciously looking for a father figure, and she found two of them, both alcoholic wife-beaters like her father. Predictably, she didn't get much love from them either. She'd tried to be a perfect child to please her father and now tried to be a perfect wife for Augustus. She dressed for him. She undressed for him. She glowed for him. She and her mother showered with him the night before their wedding (as they had done with her first husband), and she allowed him to bring home other women to play with together. At first Gloria just adored Augustus; unfortunately, so did he.

Why would anyone put up with such humiliation and abuse? Glo was afraid to leave Augustus for financial reasons, as neither was much of a success in business, and they lived mainly off the largesse of his wealthy gay "father." But it went deeper than that. Gloria was afraid of losing her *Self.* That's because, being a "Borderline Personality," she didn't have much sense of self to begin with. Borderlines are both very like and very different from narcissists. If the narcissist has an excess of ego (or at least grandiose false ego), the Borderline suffers from a lack of ego or "identity diffusion." In our earliest infantile experience, it appears that we humans actually perceive the "Good Mother" who feeds and loves us, and the "Bad Mother" who ignores, neglects, or misunderstands our needs, as two entirely separate persons. Likewise, we experience the "Good Me"—who is nurtured and protected—and the "Bad Me"—who is neglected or abused—as two separate and distinct selves. Only later are these images of the Other and of one's Self coalesced and merged into a coherent sense of a "Good Enough Mother" (not perfect, but with a preponderance of sensitive and accurate nurturing over mistakes or unavailability) and a "Good Enough Self" (not grandiose or perfect, as with the narcissist, but not inferior and inadequate either—i.e., good enough). In normal development, it's "I'm O.K., You're O.K.," just like the title of the classic text on self-esteem. But with the Borderline personality this merger never fully occurs. Thus she (Borderlines are more often female, as Narcissists are commonly male, though, again, it is unclear if this reflects an innate difference or merely the different perceptions of society and therapists) continues to perceive herself as "split" into good and bad selves. Likewise, she splits others into good guys and bad guys. For the Borderline there's no in-between. It's all black or all white, and shades of gray simply don't exist. (Just like Gloria's wardrobe.) This not only represents a severe distortion of reality, it being mostly a gray universe, but it makes it extremely hard for the Borderline to relate to people. She is constantly seeking some kind of feedback as to who the heck she *is*, and she is typically seeking it from someone she misperceives and mistrusts. The Borderline's mate finds himself worshiped, idealized, and cared for one day, then treated like a loathsome insect the next. One minute he's relating to a sexy, alluring, and doting Aphrodite, and the next he's being cursed and mauled by a serpentine Medusa. And he's done nothing different to cause this radical shift in position.

The Borderline individual lives in terror at the prospect of being abandoned and rejected, and she will go to great lengths to avoid it. For her (or him) being left alone is not only a blow to the ego, it threatens the actual loss of Self. That's because she defines herself primarily in relation to others. She's somebody's daughter, somebody's girlfriend, somebody's wife, or somebody's mother, but never just *Somebody* in her own right. She *must* have a relationship because when she's alone she doesn't know who she is.

But intimacy offers an equal and in a way identical threat for the Borderline as well. When she gets close to someone she submerges herself in him to such a degree that once again she loses any sense of her own independent self. Frightened at the threat of engulfment, she frantically backs away and/or pushes away her mate, until a safer distance is achieved. Then she fears abandonment again. Thus the Borderline's

Dilemma: to lose your Self in the Other or to lose your Self alone. Thus the Borderline's Motto: "I hate you; don't leave me."

I treated a young male borderline (which is unusual) who nicely exemplifies this pattern of relationships. He frantically pursues one girl after another, seeking instant intimacy any way he can get it. He's admittedly manipulative and deceptive, using guilt trips, "poor-me" con artistry, high-pressure courtship, and pseudo-disclosure to bag his prey. He'll say or do almost anything to please her, freely altering his persona and pretending to be someone she'll love. But once he's achieved his romantic conquest, he immediately begins to devalue her and wonder if he could do better elsewhere. He struggles to put distance between them and either is frankly unfaithful to her or may simply abandon her and move on. Having done so, he then finds that his old love looks good again, and he'll desperately seek to regain her, knowing full well that if she returns he'll dump her again. He knows he ought to abstain from all romantic involvements long enough to find a true sense of Self, but he cannot tolerate being alone. It's an exhausting roller coaster life style, but he's not quite ready to bail out just yet. Fortunately, he's also pretty bright and at heart is a decent, moral person who doesn't want to hurt anybody. Many therapists believe Borderlines can never be "cured," but he might prove them wrong.

One way of depicting the Borderline's dilemma is represented in the graph below. It shows what is called an Approach-Avoidance Gradient. The graph shows the level of fear and the intensity of desire as one approaches an object—in this case intimacy—which is both threatening and enticing. Notice that both fear and desire rise as you approach the object (intimacy) and fall off as you move away from it. The closer you get to an intimate relationship, the better it looks, and the more powerfully you are drawn to it. But when you get close to someone you open yourself up to get hurt, and this threat also grows as you approach your goal. You are tempted to cut and run, just when intimacy is about to be achieved. Notice that fear and desire rise and fall in unison, but that they are on different slopes. That is, fear rises faster and falls off quicker than attraction. Thus, at a safe distance, desire overcomes fear, and you move forward towards a more intimate relationship. As you get closer and closer, however, fear becomes stronger, and you are motivated to move back to a more comfortable distance. But then you're lonely, and the desire for intimacy takes over again. This back and forth, push-pull dance is one we all find ourselves doing at times in our lives, but it is prototypical of the Borderline's romantic attachments. It is the splitting dynamic in action, and it's hell to live with, both for the Borderline and for her mate.

The Borderline's Dilemma: an Approach-Avoidance Gradient

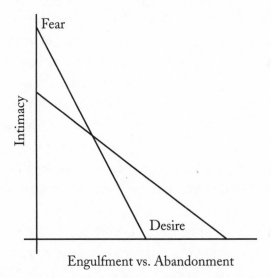

Engulfment vs. Abandonment

Life is never dull with a borderline wife. She is terrified of abandonment and begs you to stay with her, all clinging and seductive and adoring. Then she claws at your face and demands you take care of her and drives you away with her frenzied tirades. For a really graphic portrayal of this dynamic you can't beat Glenn Close's performance in the movie *Fatal Attraction*. In one especially dramatic and telling scene, she is in bed with Michael Douglas (who portrays a rather narcissistic business associate) the morning after their affair's first night. When he tries to leave for work, she complains that he *always* "runs away" after they have made love, indicating the typical borderline fear of abandonment. He tries to placate her, but she goads him into telling her off. When seductiveness fails her, she literally kicks him out of bed, claws at his shirt and cusses him out. He leaves the room and she follows in a moment, back to being coy, seductive, and sweet. He embraces her only to discover that she has slit her wrists and is bleeding all over him. It's a classic depiction of the Borderline's motto: "I hate you; don't leave me."

Borderlines and Narcissists just love each other. Well, actually, neither knows much about truly loving, but they are irresistibly drawn to each other and to the cosmic energy their relationship generates. The narcissist feels flattered by the borderline's adoring and pleasure-seeking seductiveness, which bolster his weak sense of a masculine ego. She makes him look good and feel good. She treats him (at first) like the Special One he wants to believe himself to be. Her utter dependency is also ego-inflating at first, though it becomes annoying and burdensome later. The borderline's lack of a sense of self allows the narcissist to mold and shape her as he desires (a la Pygmalian and Galatea, Augustus and Gloria), again feeding his own grandiosity. Meanwhile, she'll play with him, engage in mutual pleasure-seeking, and mother the hurt little boy inside him.

For her part, the borderline is attracted to the narcissist because he seems to have more than enough ego to share with her, thus compensating for her own lack of a coherent self-image. Narcissists appear to be strong enough to take care of all the borderline's needs, and even their rages may seem exciting to the stimulus-hungry borderline. Lacking a sense of self, borderlines feel empty inside, and they try to fill up this emptiness with food, alcohol, sex, and any other strong source of stimulation they can find. Chaotic romances fill the bill quite nicely, and affairs with narcissists are sure to be tempestuous and exciting. Narcissists will initially be proud to show off their sexy lovers, and borderlines find this flattering and provocative. Narcissists have a boyish charm about them, and they are fun to play with. Finally, the borderline can't resist wanting to mother the child-like narcissistic male. This is not, of course, a formula for concocting a stable long-term relationship.

My counseling with Gloria and Augustus started promisingly enough. They were back together after their latest separation and the battle was raging uncontrollably. They were interested in making some changes, and Lord knows the dynamics of their relationship were not difficult to analyze. Both seemed relieved and optimistic that I understood their feelings and needs and was willing to help. Of course, neither wanted to change anything except the other, but that's typical of marital therapy. Augustus was overwhelmed with Glo's complaints and hysterical diatribes. He was relieved to find that he could be a competent husband simply by listening to her sympathetically (though even this was hard for such a self-absorbed man). Glo felt a little safer with my absolute injunction against violence, having just spent $500 to repair the teeth Augustus had broken in his latest rampage. Each complained bitterly of the other's career failure and blamed the other for their own. It was troublesome getting past her histrionics and his bragging and name-dropping, but we seemed to connect reasonably well. Besides, they both loved telling me their stories and revealing the other's dirty secrets.

However, they also loved fighting, and Augustus continued to beat her up occasionally, see other women, and criticize her incessantly. Glo wanted to leave again, but feared for herself and her children. They saw another therapist briefly, with similar results. Then another friend, who'd been paying for their therapy, got disgusted with them and withdrew his support. They kept coming in, but sporadically and mostly in the midst of chaos and crisis. I was more referee and arbiter than therapist. Augustus' verbal attacks became increasingly venomous and vituperative, and his physical assaults, though infrequent, could not be tolerated. Gloria, being the brighter of the two, understood what I was telling them and tried to make changes, but couldn't resist splitting, spitting, and quitting when Augustus failed to acknowledge her efforts or to make changes himself. Then Augustus dragged "Eddie" into the therapy.

Eddie mainly muddied up the waters, pretending to be trying to save the marriage, but covertly siding with Augustus and denigrating and demonizing Gloria. He and Augustus' brother did manage to show him what a predatory beast he was and even propelled him briefly into a dramatic pseudo-conversion. "Born again," he was remorseful and morose and sought to reconcile with Gloria, who had fled to the safety of a women's shelter. But Glo, as borderlines do in severe crises, had become increasingly depressed, paranoid, and self-destructive. They reconciled briefly and relatively calmly, but it was not to last. Nor was Augustus' conversion.

I saw them only twice over the next year. They had split up and reunited several times in the interim. When last I saw them they were divorcing. She was suing him for custody, for assault, and for repayment of an old doctor bill he'd refused to cover. She was charging Eddie with molesting her children, and Eddie was suing her for slander, while publicly calling her a whore and a lesbian. The happy couple were broke, but Augustus was living off of Eddie. Most of my bill was left unpaid, with no way to collect it.

It was a good show, and I must admit I'm probably narcissistic and voyeuristic enough myself to take them on again, believing I could help. Deep down, though, I hope I know better.

At a superficial level, Borderlines and Narcissists are easy for a therapist to relate to. The borderlines tend to be attractive, sexy, seductive, and emotionally expressive. They give you a lot to work with in therapy, are responsive if not outright flirtatious, and they are desperate for your help. They do tend to cross boundaries, making "emergency" phone calls that aren't, arriving late or not showing up, being overly touchy-feely. But setting and enforcing clear therapeutic and personal limits usually heads off much of this potential uproar. Meanwhile, borderlines are people-pleasers and will mold themselves into whatever shape you most desire—temporarily. They think you are wonderful, and they tell you so—for a while.

The Narcissists tend to be highly intelligent, well-educated, successful, and charming. They are doctors, lawyers, politicians, CEOs of large, profitable companies. They are knowledgeable and often powerful people who are delighted to share with you (i.e., show off) what they know. After all, the narcissist is trying to live up to a grandiose self-image and prove to the world how superior he is. Many of them very nearly achieve the greatness they seek or pretend to have. It can be quite flattering to have one's advice sought out by such an impressive person, at least until one recognizes that for all his praise and flattery, the narcissist does not see you as a real person. You're only a great doctor because such a great patient could have no other kind. In a sense, you feel reduced to an image as well.

Therapy with borderline and narcissistic couples is sure to become chaotic and exciting, which is to say troublesome, sooner or later. Narcissists are hypersensitive to criticism and can be extremely hot-tempered. Borderlines tend to criticize and belittle as part of their splitting process. When they verbally attack their spouses, the reaction may be a physical assault. Narcissists are highly competitive guys; many compete with their wives as well as their professional adversaries. If the wife shows him up, he may reduce her to a manageable size with his fists. Thus, I saw a brain surgeon who gave his wife a concussion when she questioned his selection of a bottle of wine. I saw a financial planner, the regional manager for a national firm, who could not tolerate his wife's success in business. She was a vice president for a start-up software company which went from local to international in mere months. Her income soared into orbit, and her stock options went inter-galactic, her total wealth eclipsing his own considerable portfolio. He became so angry he blackened her eye, split her lip, and filed for divorce. Only when her company went nova and filed for Chapter 13 did he find her loveable again and seek a reconciliation. He *knew* he was being silly, small-minded, and egotistical, but he couldn't help himself. He also got so mad at a vociferous supporter of a rival football team that mistakenly trounced Alabama that he punched the guy out at the stadium. He spent the night in jail and was nearly fired from his job. He lost his self-respect and that of his wife. But he was so ego-involved with Alabama athletics that the team's defeat was truly his own and therefore intolerable. (Actually, this is a pretty common phenomenon in Alabama, and not unheard of elsewhere.) A few beers hadn't helped his self-control much either.

He was scared and chagrined, his wife furious. It made for several entertaining hours of therapy.

Narcissists have such fragile egos and so little impulse control that they are easily tempted by an attractive female, especially another borderline. They love to be pampered and praised and adored. Thus, they are quite likely to have extramarital affairs or engage in various other sexual misconducts, which also spices up the marital therapy. For the narcissist, affairs are mostly about ego. Though some delude themselves with the romantic notion they are in love, what they are really seeking is the ego-boost of someone finding them attractive and devoting exclusive attention to them. The lover is only a vehicle by which the narcissist tries to love himself. There is very little that could be called a relationship. In a sense, the affair is actually autoerotic.

The best-known example of this may come directly from the Oval Office of the White House. "Bill" was bright enough to become a Rhodes Scholar, but this was evidently not enough to overcome the inferiority he felt at being abandoned by his mother (who left him with his grandparents after his father's death) and growing up on the wrong side of Hope, Arkansas. He determined as a schoolboy to become President, but that wasn't enough either, especially as many of his grandiose plans fizzled on the launching pad. So he pursued a series of affairs, all with "bimbos" in some way inferior to him (and therefore not threatening to him). Notice that these do not appear to have been love matches in any real sense, or even to involve much in the way of a mutual relationship. Bill didn't even try to meet "Monica's" sexual or emotional needs. Instead, he had her on her knees, worshipping at his private parts. It wasn't about love or romance, or even primarily about sex; it was about Bill's inflated ego.

Similarly, I had occasion to work with another narcissistic politician, coincidentally also an international scholar who had known President Clinton—a fact he mentioned twice in our first interview (along with his high six-figure income). His wife had taken him back after his first affair, even though he gave her a disease. Now she found he was keeping a mistress in an expensive apartment. He thought that he was in love with the woman and fancied himself her rescuer and protector. Actually the woman was essentially a prostitute, using his money and cheating on him on the side, but the "rescuer" role flattered his narcissism, and the deceitfulness of the affair made him feel crafty and superior. He revealed in therapy that he'd had at least a dozen other affairs. Clearly, this wasn't about love; it was about ego.

A bit surprisingly, for a narcissist and small-scale philanderer, "Horatio" was a quiet, soft-spoken, almost self-effacing gentleman. Pleasant-looking, but certainly not overly handsome, with a bit of a middle-aged spread and incipiently graying hair, Horatio wasn't concerned with his physical image. His grandiosity was tied up in legislation and litigation, and there he was Apollo, the Sun God. In his political career he had championed the cause of the down-trodden, the victimized, the forgotten; and he'd won the day for them. And for himself, which is where his mega-house, speed boat, and fancy cars had come from. But that wasn't enough for Horatio.

Neither was his wife, though "Daphne" was a raven-haired Greek goddess who should have been enough for any man. Approaching midlife when I knew her, she could still turn heads. She was a devoted wife and nurturing mother who knew how to play (though she'd had little chance lately) and who knew how to work (part-time, as a nurse) and who had cleverly and tastefully designed and decorated the million-plus house Horatio had lusted after. But Horatio had other lusts which had nothing to do with Daphne.

Amazingly, my politician either had or developed something of a conscience, or perhaps he just realized that he'd lose his career, his show house, his reputation, and his family if he didn't quit messing around. He gave up his paramour and tossed her out of their love nest, then sold it. He took an oath of fidelity (not for the first time) and seemed dedicated to keeping it (for the first time). He devoted himself to his wife and rediscovered what a fun, attractive, bright, and loving person he'd married. Still more amazingly, this incredible woman forgave him again. His capacity for betrayal was simply outmatched by her capacity to forgive. He began to see himself as a good father and faithful, loving husband, a considerably less grandiose self-image than that of Rescuer, but one which was based in reality and plenty "good enough" to live with. Last I heard they were still together and doing fine. They may make it.

My next narcissistic adulterer was not so successful. A "lay minister" in his church, "Perseus," devoted increasing amounts of time to a prison ministry, preaching to and counseling with convicted felons. (His real name was actually "Percy," but he thought that too plebeian and dressed it up with the Greek version instead.) He particularly enjoyed his work with the female prisoners, who seemed especially impressed with his oratory and grateful for his attention. His relationship with a lady embezzler (or so he thought her) quickly developed into a torrid love affair, which continued after her release. Like my politico, Perseus saw himself as a knight in armor, rescuing this poor damsel in distress and putting her up in her own little castle (another condo, which he could ill afford). He too agreed with my diagnosis and description of his narcissism, even recognizing that his ministry was not for God's glory but for his own. His wife D'Anna was also willing to take him back and forgive him, despite his continued lies and infidelities—and his prior history of affairs. Yet he could not give up his mistress, even when he found out she had several other boyfriends and had actually been in prison for drugs and prostitution. He just couldn't forgo the ego boost he got from the adoration of this manipulative, deceitful, immoral, and frankly low-class woman. As is often the case in such affairs, the other woman was nothing to look at either, while the wife was quite nicely put together. There's no lie like the lie you tell to yourself.

The other sexual misconduct I often find associated with pathological narcissism is addictive pornography, the couch-potato's answer to compulsive philandering. It is the ultimate demonstration that narcissism is a distorted, twisted form of self-love. A moderately obese, balding research chemist was married to a nice, but obsessive woman whose gynecological problems strained their marital relationships. Convincing himself that his wife didn't want to have sex, he rationalized that he was doing her a favor by meeting his own needs elsewhere. Over ten years or so he spent nearly twenty thousand dollars on pornography and topless bars. As with any addiction, he found that his need increased the more he satisfied it. He became an obsessive collector of videos, magazines, and books, and as he became increasingly jaded, his taste ran to ever more bizarre, perverse, and grotesque material. Gross, gaping genitalia, women with animals, even books featuring excremental sex. Nothing was too hard-core, except pedophilia. A loving father, he refused to buy materials involving children. On business trips he hung out at topless joints and got a huge ego boost from looking at and then talking with the dancers—but as a kind of father-protector, not a potential sex partner. (Again we see the rescuer fantasy at work.) In fact he had no affairs, no actual sexual contact with anyone outside his marriage. Yet he finally realized that he was in truth unfaithful to his wife. He had invested his sexuality and his emotional intimacy outside his marriage, where it belonged, and that's infidelity. He also realized that his relationships with go-go girls were largely phony and self-serving. Finally, he found that his sexuality was utterly self-focused. Pornography is not a relationship with a girl in a movie; it is autoeroticism. The picture is a vehicle to help one masturbate. Woody Allen said, "Don't knock masturbation; at least it's sex with someone I love." But pornography addiction isn't even true self-love. It's only loving oneself in a distorted way, the way of narcissism. This is what I tried to help his wife understand. Her husband's pornography addiction wasn't about her at all, except that it pulled him further away from her. It was all about narcissistic ego-building and the substitution of pleasure-seeking for truly being happy with oneself.

Utterly disgusted with himself, my porno addict gave it up entirely, dumping over 500 pounds of lurid videos and licentious magazines at the county landfill (which no doubt greatly accelerated the composting process). He soon found he'd lost all interest in dirty pictures, though he did kind of miss his fatherly chats with his buxom pseudo-daughters. His wife suffered a major bout of depression, much of it concerning her own self-esteem issues, but stuck by him and saved the marriage. He came in periodically for a reality check and to update me on his crazy family's latest escapades. We've figured that his narcissism probably stems from a critical, demanding father and a seductive, image-conscious, but rejecting mother. His obsession with looking at the nude female form probably began with his older sister exposing herself to him beginning when he was ten (she was sixteen) and continuing even into middle age. His "hoarding" or obsessive collecting probably relates to his mother's tendency to refuse her children various privileges or gifts on an entirely capricious and unfair basis. The sister who relates to him erotically has had a series of affairs with married men, but has never married. She dotes on the sociopath she adopted as a son. Another sister married a bisexual. Several siblings are obsessed with psychics and "channeling," and messages from their deceased relatives. My guy is easily the sanest of the bunch and has learned to be happy with his wife, his children, and himself. He's rejected the negative self-image imposed on him by his family but also his grandiose fantasies of rescuing beautiful girls. He sees himself now simply as an okay guy, and that's good enough for him. It's also the cure for narcissism. Reject both extremes, both the inadequate, incompetent Self and the grandiose false Self, and adopt the middle position. Learn to like yourself on a realistic basis, for simply being okay. It's a little depressing to relinquish your grandiosity but it leaves you with a reality-based, yet positive self-image. And that's "good enough." Unfortunately, most narcissistic personalities can't do it. My lay preacher couldn't, and Augustus never came close.

Writers and cinematographers love narcissists and borderlines because they lead such colorful and dramatic lives, especially as they relate to each other. Movies and books abound with depictions of these character disorders. Tolstoy's Anna Karenina is a Borderline to Count Vronsky's Narcissist. So probably are Katherina and Petruchio in Shakespeare's *The Taming of the Shrew*. In Hemingway's *The Sun Also Rises*, Brett is quite the borderline, while *all* her men are narcissistic, except perhaps the narrator. Scarlett O' Hara could have invented borderlinism, and Rhett Butler pushed narcissism nearly to its extreme form of sociopathy. But *Fatal Attraction* still edges out *Gone with the Wind* as far as cinematic portrayals of narcissistic/borderline relationships is concerned. Tom Cruise is a good actor, but he seems pretty narcissistic in films like *Top Gun* and *The Firm* and *Mission Impossible*, and even in his more sympathetic role in *Rain Man*.

Why are artistic depictions of borderlines and narcissists so common and so popular? Perhaps it is because these individuals exemplify in dramatic fashion something universal in human relationships. Maybe we *all* have some borderline and narcissistic tendencies, and we see ourselves more clearly by viewing more extreme exemplars of these characteristics. Are these literary/cinematic portrayals of such interest because they simply exaggerate what is present and must be resisted in all of us? Do "personality disorders" really exist as "diseases," or are they merely far out on a spectrum of behavior patterns we all grapple with? I'm checking the box marked "All of the above."

CHAPTER 12

A Child of God

MULTIPLE PERSONALITY DISORDER (NOW CALLED "Dissociative Identity Disorder") has been a mysterious, controversial, and absolutely fascinating psychiatric phenomenon. My own experience with "MPD" nicely parallels that of the psychiatric field in general. That is, I practiced nearly fifteen years without seeing a single case, then suddenly found myself overrun with them, for a while treating four or five cases at a time. Then they all disappeared again. MPD was long considered extremely rare; you could practice a lifetime without seeing a single MPD patient. The disorder was known to most therapists only from textbooks, and mainly from the classic (but in some ways atypical) cases of "Eve" and later "Sybil." Then the field was suddenly flooded with them and everybody was treating at least one. Books were written; workshops were given; television and movies were obsessed with them. A huge controversy sprang up over whether MPD really existed, whether memories could really be repressed then recovered, or whether therapists might themselves be *creating* MPDs, either unwittingly or perhaps by cunning design and manipulation. Fortunes and reputations, and a lot of noise, were made. Then the MPD wellspring dried up. My last new case was almost twenty years ago. So what really happened?

Frankly, I'm not sure what to think. I have no doubt that my MPD patients, at least most of them, truly experienced themselves as split into multiple parts or persons. They weren't just acting. Not even Meryl

Streep or Helen Mirren could play so many different roles so consistently and so convincingly for such a long time. In my opinion they were sincere. Some of them were treatment-wise when I met them and knew a great deal about MPD. They could have faked it or have been therapist-induced cases. But others were quite naive and would not have known how to mimic this disorder if they wanted to. One of my patients knew nothing of MPD, had never even heard of it. Her name was Wanda, and she was a poor, uneducated African-American woman from rural Alabama. At age forty she was driving happily along a country highway when suddenly she turned to her sister and asked her to stop the car and take the wheel. When her sister asked why, she answered in a panic, "Because I'm only nine years old and I don't know how to drive." She had spontaneously "switched" to an alternate personality, herself at age nine. When I questioned her later in the hospital, forty-year-old Wanda switched again, and nine-year-old Wanda told me of having been violently raped by two neighbors as a child. Unable to live with this memory, Wanda had created another personality to hold and contain it. To the age of forty the main personality had no recall for these rapes and no awareness of her alter ego, but the memory was starting to come back. She was extremely distressed, not to mention very confused about her new-found, long-lost nine-year-old self. Nine-year-old Wanda left me a note that nicely revealed her state of mind, as well as her naivete and lack of education. It certainly did not seem faked to me.

Besides, what motivation might lie beneath the counterfeit production of MPD? Did these women endure hospital stays, mutilate themselves, take dangerous medications, spend endless hours in therapy, and run up huge bills just to get my attention? Anybody who can pay my hourly fee can *have* my attention. Did they do these things to torment their families? Some had no contact with their families, while others had very close, supportive family relationships. While MPDs can be pretty passive-aggressive, I doubt this as the primary motivator for most of them. But if Multiple Personality Disorder is a real, legitimate psychiatric disorder, where has it been all our lives, and where (and why) did it go away? I can't give a definitive answer. Historically, mental illnesses do tend to vary considerably in terms of relative frequencies and intensities. "Hysteria," for example, has nearly disappeared because people are too aware of its psychological basis to take it at face value. In Freud's day it was extremely common, but I've seen only one true hysterical blindness or paralysis, and that in a naive thirteen-year-old farm girl. Similarly, anorexia seems to come and go, varying partly with the level of adolescent anxiety in our society and partly with what insurance companies will cover. Bulimia was unheard of thirty years ago, had its run, and still occurs, though less frequently. The current fad illnesses are ADHD and personality disorders such as narcissism or borderlinism, with bipolar disorder making a strong bid for taking over first place. Was MPD just another fad, hyped by the media and over-eager clinicians and now consigned to the museum of ancient illnesses? I don't know. But I do know my own experiences with MPD patients have been among the most meaningful, challenging, rewarding, and confusing of my career.

They began with "June," though we were well along in therapy before either of us knew of her multiplicity. June was a tall, slender, attractive woman of forty when she first consulted me about her depression and panic problems. She was accompanied at times by her husband Ward, a great bear of a man (though definitely more of the Teddy than Grizzly variety). I got June on some medication and taught her how to control her panic disorder with breathing and muscle relaxation, distraction, and re-thinking exercises. Then we set about dealing with the stressors that had pushed her into depression. The most immediate of these were "Willie" and "The Beaver," her adolescent children. Willie was a nineteen-year-old theater student with long purple hair and a hankering for bad boys and booze. She was in danger of flunking out of college because she was mostly drinking and studying the anatomy of "Eddie," a shy pot-head with a nose ring and a blue Mohawk haircut (which shaded into a sickly green towards the blond roots.) At thirteen her brother "Beaver" was eager to follow in her rebellious footsteps and had a good start with cigarettes and a few stolen CDs. June was doing her best to provide discipline and guidance but was getting very little help from her Teddy Bear husband. That placed stress on the marriage, adding to her anxiety and depression.

I got June and Ward together and negotiated a new penal code for the children. Willie came to see me on her own and was clearly depressed and confused herself. She no longer enjoyed her acting, as her rigid, dictatorial professors and their onerous assignments had turned it from fun into drudgery. Suddenly her career choice loomed like a prison sentence. She wasn't really that excited about Eddie, either, but she was generally afraid of men, and Eddie was safe and controllable. Her depression, it appeared, stemmed from having been sexually abused by her uncle, June's half-brother, though it was certainly exacerbated by drugs and alcohol. That was the revelation that rocked the family and ultimately led to the discovery of June's MPD.

Willie responded well to medication and counseling, dropping Eddie and switching her major to child education. As she processed the childhood molestation, she was able to conquer her shame and rebuild her self-esteem. She no longer needed the excitement and distraction of drugs, sex, and liquor. She eventually graduated and became a school teacher, which she loved, pursuing her acting in community theater groups. But the cat was out of the bag now and June's therapeutic journey was only beginning.

The focus at first was on straightening out the kids, which required that June and Ward resolve their marital problems. Then Willie's allegations of abuse led to an exploration of the broader family dynamics, and that's when things began to get weird. June's parents were outraged at the attack on their son and vehemently denied the alleged abuse. They came in to see me for a family session and strongly defended their family and denounced our therapy, even threatening me with a law suit (not for the last time). June's father was a sleazy little con artist, door-to-door salesman, and compulsive gambler. They'd had to move at least twice in June's childhood to avoid the Mob on the one hand and the Law on the other. Her mother had left him at least once and had herself been hospitalized under the stress of his nefarious activities. June's mother was a Carrie Nation—style crusader and fancied herself a lay missionary, ministering and preaching to prisoners, the homeless, and other unfortunates. She was rigid, puritanical, calculating, and defensive, and apparently had good reason to be so. There was no abuse in *her* family, she declared, and Willie was making it all up.

But a closer look at family issues got June to remembering her own past, and as she did she began to reexamine her family life from a new perspective. She remembered her mother locking her and her sister in the closet for hours at a time and tying her to the bed, mouth taped shut, as punishment for back talk. Wasn't that "abuse?" (It was.) A talk with her sister confirmed the accuracy of this memory, and indeed Mother admitted to the events, while denying they constituted abuse. And June's sister also remembered being sexually abused as a child, which had led to her own problems with depression. June began to remember long lonely days of childhood neglect while Father ran his scams and Mother pampered a series of foster children, especially the half-uncle who molested Willie. Her "good Christian family" looked less and less loving as she allowed herself to look honestly at events she'd long refused to consider.

When you deprive someone of his historical background, his past, you take away his sense of his own identity. That's what Alex Haley was talking about in *Roots* and Bob Marley was singing about in "Buffalo Soldiers." And that's what happened to June when her family roots were proven rotten and false. At first she merely seemed to be in an identity crisis. She was dissatisfied with her marriage and her career and her appearance. She began to change her hairstyle and color and to buy different clothes and act for all the world like an adolescent. She rebelled against anything her husband wanted, stayed out late, and hung out with new, younger friends. Ward came to me almost in despair, not knowing how to deal with a wife he didn't recognize, who changed dramatically from one day to the next. I explained the identity crisis and adolescent behavior (what all people do in an identity crisis) as temporary and recommended he relax, not to take it too seriously, and try to enjoy himself. He was living the dream of every middle-aged man—to be romantically involved with a teenaged girl. He wasn't much reassured, but he did admit their sex life had gotten better.

Then June's mood darkened and her crisis deepened. She'd long protected her image of herself and family by refusing to see them accurately and running from the memories of her childhood. She had compulsively distracted herself with working and parenting, and her panic attacks, while highly distressing, had effectively detoured old memories. Now her defenses were breaking down, and the memories were returning, along with the painful, angry, and shameful feelings attached to them. June was overwhelmed as new visions of herself began to flood her consciousness, first in dreams, later in waking "flashbacks." She began to re-experience episodes from her childhood as if they were happening *now*. And they were episodes of abuse. We were in the second year of June's therapy now, and she did not know who she was or exactly what had happened to her, but she suspected it was pretty awful, and she was scared to find out. We had no idea then just how bad it would turn out to be.

June called me one morning in a panic and had to come in at once. When she arrived she was like a child, crying, shaking uncontrollably, glancing about fearfully, barely able to talk. She cowered in a corner and stared at me until her eyes went out of focus and she somehow detached. She then went into a flashback, re-experiencing and acting out an episode of childhood sexual abuse. In the future we would find that if I sat with her on the floor and held onto her hand it gave her enough contact with present reality to avoid being totally swallowed by the past. This first time, however, I could only sit powerlessly until the episode was over. June was exhausted and depressed and terrified of remembering more. She wanted to die. I put her in the hospital to be sure she didn't, the first of many admissions to come. In the hospital she again "dissociated," either into flashbacks or simply going into a trance. Her condition and our therapy had escalated to a whole new level, heralded by the appearance of her dissociative episodes. Dissociation, after all, is the hallmark of MPD.

Dissociation is a defense mechanism, a way of protecting oneself from an awful reality by disconnecting from it. It is considered a "primitive" defense because it so strongly denies reality, but in mild form it is normal and not uncommon. It comes in different forms and is available to most of us only in extreme circumstances. A fairly common dissociation is the lack of emotion and altered sense of time experienced in an automobile accident. I once hit an oil slick doing about 65 mph, turned several 360s and slid backwards into the median, where I stuck fast in mud to the floorboard. A truck driver stopped and asked if I needed help and said, "You sure put on a helluva show there, Buddy." "You shoulda been watching from my seat," I grinned back. The point is, I never felt scared, and I experienced the whole incident in a detached, slow-motion fashion, as if I was merely watching a movie. I was dissociated or disconnected from a normal emotional reaction, and in a sense, from reality. It all seemed quite unreal, a form of dissociation called "de-realization."

Similarly, victims of childhood sexual abuse often describe the event in the third person, as if they'd happened to someone else. Many describe the abuse from the vantage point of the ceiling or from within a wall. It's as if they watched rather than experienced the molestation. That's a dissociative reaction called "depersonalization." The abuse was real, but it didn't happen to *me*. The ultimate in dissociation is to go one step further: the abuse didn't happen to me; it happened to someone else. And that is what MPDs appear to be doing. They take the abuse experience and isolate it from the rest of their memory, separating it from their consciousness and encapsulating it safely away. They split off a portion of their awareness, which is to say, of *themselves*, and create a new, alternative self to experience and remember the abuse. This new "personality" co-exists with the primary personality and comes into play, at first, only in abuse situations. The main personality is protected from the abuse because she doesn't experience or remember it. The "alter" does. Of course, for the trick to work, it is also necessary to forget the existence of the alter. That's why new MPD patients don't know they have the disorder. But the alter continues to exist and to act autonomously at times, often behaving in ways foreign to the main (or "core" or "host") personality. This could include promiscuous sex, binge eating, suicidal or self-mutilating behavior, or perhaps just buying clothes in a totally different style. Whatever it is, this puzzling, often troubling, independent action is what brings the multiple into therapy.

June entered therapy because she was depressed and experiencing severe panic attacks. After dealing with marital and family problems, we now began to discover what the panic was all about. June had a remarkable memory, very detailed and extending all the way back to her second or third year of life. Most people's memory begins at age four or five, but June either remembered back to her crib or remembered descriptions of it from others. Her memories were confirmed by her mother and older sister. Yet there were big gaps when she recalled little or nothing, as if her memory for these times had been erased. Actually, they'd been blocked, not blotted out, and as we began to explore her past, June began to remember more and more of it. Often she'd have a dream, hinting at some abusive or traumatic event from her early childhood. She'd awaken in a panic, call me, then come in to discuss it. In the office she'd dissociate and experience the event in a flashback. Her panic attacks were her fear of remembering horrible episodes of childhood abuse. As these came faster and faster, she was unable to process and contain them, and she feared they'd overwhelm her and drive her insane. I assured her this could not happen, since these were events she'd already experienced without going insane, *as a small child*. With adult coping skills she could deal with them even more effectively and without dissociating. But this was scant comfort in the face of a flood of horrible memories. Sometimes only the hospital could calm her and make her feel safe again. And the memories kept coming.

June had always remembered being tied down or locked up by her mother, as well as her mother's sarcastic criticism and verbal abuse and her father's sleazy manipulations. Now she began to feel that she'd been sexually abused as well, and increasingly she came to believe that her father was somehow involved. She remembered herself as a four-year-old, wearing a white gown and lying rigidly between several other children, trying to hide and dreading to be the next one "selected." She remembered a lovely lady, dressed and acting like Donna Reed, trying unsuccessfully to comfort and soothe her—and warning her what could happen if she protested. She remembered a boy with brown skin and black hair and eyes who did protest and was loaded into a barrel and dumped into the water to drown. Bit by bit she remembered a warehouse on the waterfront, large crates, some with snakes in them, which were used to scare her and the other children. She remembered bright lights and cameras and men and women watching and then she remembered them doing things to her and making her do things. Fondling, licking, sucking things. With other girls and boys. With men. With animals and snakes. She remembered trying to hide, lying very still and pretending not to be there, not to be experiencing these awful events, wishing they were happening to someone else. And so they did.

By the end of our second year of therapy, June's dissociative episodes were coming more and more frequently and had begun to take a different form. She continued to "lose time" and to have "flashbacks," but she also began to "switch" to other personalities. She'd long kept a daily journal, and now she began to show me passages in a totally different handwriting from her own, passages she did not remember writing. Some of them were signed with other names, crying out for comfort and describing other traumas from her childhood. In our sessions she continued to have flashbacks but now also to take on other personas and speak in the voices of her "alters." It was subtle at first, but I began to recognize these others, to detect the changes in facial expression, intonation, and manner of speaking. Each of the alters had a story to tell, and gradually they revealed the extent of the massive, incredible abuse they'd endured. Together, June and I literally descended into Hell, with her other selves as our guides.

MPDs create their alternate personalities by copying what they know and see around them. They imagine and construct alters who are strong enough to take the abuse without complaint or who are too weak to protest or who perhaps are mute and therefore unable to speak out. Some of them are other child personalities, but others quite commonly are parents, both good and bad ones. They can be any age or sex and may even be personified spirits rather than humans. "Death" is not an uncommon alter, and "Good Mother" is nearly universal. They are often modeled after real people, "Bad Mother," for example—but, with a child's inability to distinguish fantasy from reality, may come right out of a storybook or a TV sitcom. "Little Miss" and "Missy" are pretty popular.

In addition to "June" herself, the dominant or "host" or "core" personality, June's cast of characters included at least five others:

1. A child personality, representative of the three-year-old June, had experienced and held the memories of the worst of the abuse. Pretty, fearful, and naive, we came to think of her as "Little Miss." She saw herself as tiny and usually clothed in a white nightgown.

2. A boy child, somewhat resembling the Mexican boy she remembered, but never clearly named, never fully "out" in our sessions, and poorly differentiated from Little Miss. He reintegrated pretty quickly with the other child alter and disappeared.

3. "Prudence" was modeled largely after June's mother. Rigid, obsessive-compulsive, and moralistic, Prudence labored to make June perfect in order to make her acceptable to her parents and thereby protect her from further abuse. Having met June's mother myself, I recognized Prudence at once, though she wasn't nearly so self-righteous, hypocritical, or cold as the real thing. Once toned down and turned positive, she was a real asset to June in everyday life.

4. "The '50s Lady" was June's attempt to create a good mother in the midst of abuse, especially the child pornography alluded to above. She never revealed any other name, but she was a classic 1950's TV Mom, an amalgamation of Donna Reed, Harriet Nelson, and June Cleaver (actress Barbara Billingsley). She appears from June's memories to have been based on a real person, who helped calm and comfort the children used in pornographic films and photos. She was as close as June got in those days to a vision of a sympathetic, loving mother. She also represented a major aspect of

June's personality, as she was herself a loving mother and in some ways was rather old-fashioned and conservative as well. The '50s Lady had her dark, sneaky side (after all, she was in league with the pornographers) but was very much a "protective alter." In therapy she was very helpful in soothing the terrified child alters, as they trusted her implicitly.

5. Based on her real father, "The Mocker" was a sleazy, manipulative, deceitful, and cynical con artist. As June increasingly understood the depth of her father's involvement in her abuse, the Mocker became more and more powerful and abusive, tormenting June and the other alters, mocking and teasing them, telling June she was a slut and a whore, and driving her towards suicide. June feared the Mocker though she was also entranced by his evil power.

Almost nothing about Multiple Personality Disorder is noncontroversial, even to its very existence as a psychiatric disorder. What has become the "standard model" of MPD—if there is any—says that its divided personality structure is maintained by barriers of amnesia. A new "alter" personality is created to experience the abuse, and the primary personality "represses" or forgets all memory of the trauma. It then forgets having created the alter, forgets the existence of the alter, and forgets, or never knows, what the alter does when he or she "comes out" and takes over control of the body and its consciousness. Typically there are several alters and sometimes dozens of them, all separated from awareness of each other by varying barriers of amnesia. What eventually emerges can be an enormously complex structure of alters and memories with varying degrees of consciousness, varying awareness of each other, and varying degrees of contact between them. The alters may communicate with each other in written messages (written in a communal diary or perhaps carved into the body's own flesh), via internal hallucinatory "voices," or simply by acting in strange ways and leaving clues behind. MPDs may become aware of their multiplicity by experiencing "lost time," periods of hours or even days for which they have no memory. These are times when another alter is in control.

The primary personality discovers the products of a shopping spree in her closet, notices the drop in the car's gas gauge, or perhaps wakes up with wrists cut and bleeding. Another of my MPD patients woke up half way across the state with a ten-inch switchblade knife on the car seat beside her. She had no idea how she'd gotten there or how she'd obtained the impressive and illegal weapon. The same patient (described below as "Dorothy") was extremely frightened and disgusted by sex. A mischievous and promiscuous alter delighted in picking up a man in a bar, climbing into bed with him, then switching maliciously back to the main personality to deal with him.

In these complex MPD cases there are levels upon levels of consciousness, memory, and ego states. Alter A may have only the vaguest clue as to her own multiple self-structure, but may be partially aware of Alter B. Alter B knows everything about A but can communicate clearly only with Alter C and doesn't even know of D—who is the master "controller," who knows about and can contact *everybody*. Therapy is all about reconnecting and reintegrating these parts of a fractured self. It is about breaking down the memory barriers between them so that all the alters know what each remembers (just as a normal person has access to all her memory banks and personality traits). This is a painful process because it means remembering not only what happened but how it felt. It is terrifying as well, both because of fear of the still unknown traumas and because therapy takes away the defense mechanisms of repression and dissociation. The patient feels helpless and alone in the face of utter terror and hideous pain. Naturally, she resists, memory by memory, alter by alter. She tries to hide her multiplicity, hide her various selves, cover up the awful memories. She uses distraction, uproar, acting-out, deceptiveness, and the very complexity of the personality system itself to keep the therapist, and more importantly, herself, from uncovering the truth.

The goal is for the therapist to connect in turn with each part of the patient's consciousness, develop a trusting relationship, and help her (or him) tell of and process her traumatic story. Then, each alter is encouraged to share with the others and to give and receive comfort and support. As the alters talk and share with each other, each takes away some of the other's memory and awareness and consequently becomes a bit more like the other. Eventually the two are indistinguishable, as they have merged or integrated into one consciousness, one Self. This can happen step by step, with various subgroups of alters until all are re-integrated, beginning, for example, with all the child alters or all the mother figures. It's slow, painful, and complicated work, with lots of surprises and setbacks and always the risk of suicide. It's not for the faint-hearted or impatient or those lacking in imagination or flexibility. In a single one-hour session the therapist may talk with several alters, as the patient spontaneously switches to one, who may be asked to call out another, who may be forcibly superseded by an intrusive third. Some alters pretend to be others or won't reveal their identity; some don't even know. Alters are jealous of each other and of the therapist's time and attention. Some want to destroy or emasculate others. Some—the most dangerous—won't talk out their feelings, but insist on acting them out in suicidal, self-destructive, or aggressive behaviors.

Relatively speaking, June's case actually proceeded pretty smoothly, though I wouldn't have said so at the time. June remembers her therapy as two years of terror, nearly constant urges to suicide, and repeated, painful hospital stays. It was also a time of tremendous self-discovery, marital growth, and the forming of close friendships. It was a time of reopening but also finally of healing old wounds. I doubt that most people have the courage, tenacity, and integrity required to complete the process, but June did.

As best we could reconstruct it from her recovered memories, here's June's incredible story:

At age three her father sold June's services to a child pornography ring, probably to pay off gambling debts. She was repeatedly fondled, sodomized, and forced to perform oral sex on children and adults of both genders. She was filmed in sexual encounters with animals, terrorized with snakes, and perhaps forced to witness the execution of another child (although this may well have been faked to intimidate the other children). Her father was initially an observer but later became involved in molesting June himself.

The first of her abusers, the pornographers, were presumably connected with organized crime. But then June's father fell in with some sort of Satanic cult, and the abuse got much worse. June remembered being stripped and shoved to her knees in a circle of other children. She was forced to participate in sexual activities and to torture other children, and they were made to believe they were drinking human blood. Finally, she was actually placed in a coffin and briefly buried. She was forced to take drugs, apparently with hallucinogenic properties, presumably to confuse her and alter her state of consciousness. She was exhumed and told she'd died and gone to Hell and was now the daughter of Satan. She was given a new name to signify her new status and her membership in the cult, and she was warned if she ever told this story, she'd be killed with her husband and children.

Did all this really happen? Are people capable of such cruelty and sadism? June believes it did, and surely the Holocaust and the Trade Tower bombings teach us that no act is so heinous that some human won't do it to another. Do Satanic cults really exist, and if so, do Satanists truly engage in human sacrifice, cannibalism, and ritualized abuse? My admittedly meager research suggests that such cults do exist, although they are probably rare, and that some few may indeed perform rituals like those described by my patient. Law enforcement officials take different views, but some have told me that even central Alabama is actually noted for the existence of Satanic groups, much less Southern California. Other of my patients have described similar, though generally less gruesome, rituals. Can any of June's story be authenticated or verified?

Actually, such parts of the story as are subject to fairly ready confirmation have indeed been verified. June's sister and daughter both confirm that they too were molested. Her mother admits to the lock-ups and tie-downs, though she sees them as appropriate discipline. Her father's gambling, con artistry, and forced relocations are a matter of record. The warehouse on the water fits with her family having lived on the Southern California Coast, where a Mexican boy would have been easy enough to come by. June's mother was indeed hospitalized for depression, leaving her father access to June and sufficient time to carry out the abuse without being discovered. Her mother and sister also verify the accuracy of June's non-abuse-related memories, going all the way back to her crib. And one memory all three agree on is that even as a child June used to pretend to be, and carry on as, "California Cassie," whom they describe as a perfect 1950s housewife and mother. Was this a child's hint at her own multiplicity, a brief glimpse of the "'50s Lady?" Or was it the first efforts of a fledgling actress, later to portray herself as a multiple personality? Is there any difference in the two?

Memory is at best a highly fallible record of past events. It is often vague and spotty, frequently quite inaccurate and often missing altogether. We don't record the event itself, but only our own *perception* of it, which may be quite erroneous. This is especially true for childhood events, as children have little understanding and no perspective on many happenings. Memory changes over time, fading into misty obscurity or being clarified, and perhaps enhanced, as it is reviewed and updated with a more mature, informed perspective. It is quite possible to misattribute to memory events which occurred only in fantasy or in fiction. I think I remember telling you to pick up the car, but in fact I only remember my *imagining* that I told you. I was talking with my mother about a childhood memory which was really quite clear in my mind. "You don't remember that," she said. I insisted that I did. "You couldn't, " she replied, "because you weren't there." I guess I'd heard the story so many times as a child that I recorded it as my own memory, complete with my own embellishments to it.

Could this kind of misattribution explain the MPD accounts of abuse so vile and so extraordinary as to be unbelievable? Are these merely fantasies incorporated as if the memory of real events? Surely no one could come to believe falsely that they'd experienced such trauma. Yet Psychologist David Schacter, in *The Seven Sins of Memory*, records a well-documented example of just a spectacular misattribution of memory. In 1996 Binjimin Wilkomirski published *Fragments*, a graphic and moving account of his childhood internment in a Nazi concentration camp. The memoir achieved international recognition and praise, until a Swiss journalist found incontrovertible proof that Wilkomirski, born Bruno Doessekker, spent all of the war years with his foster parents in Switzerland. His tales of unspeakable horrors may have been true for somebody, but not for him; he was never in a camp. Yet Wilkomirski insists to this day that his memories are real and valid. Dr. Schacter believes he isn't lying, just mistaken. Are MPDs, with their "recovered memories" of Satanic abuse, similarly mistaken? Wilkomirski too had been unaware of his "past" until the memories were uncovered in psychotherapy.

Isn't it possible that June's "recovered memories" were all fabricated for my benefit or were perhaps implanted by me? It's a possibility I've considered a thousand times and one that was of great concern to me at the time of June's therapy. But I think not. Certainly I did not purposely or consciously create or encourage the development of a multiple personality disorder. For the first year or more of therapy it never occurred to me that June had MPD, and I knew very little about it, much less how to induce it. I wouldn't know *now* how to induce MPD. I had another patient where I did suspect MPD and encouraged relaxation exercises and journaling which might have revealed or suggested it. Nothing happened. Even when June did begin to remember forgotten abuse, I figured we were finished when the pornography, which is well known to exist and therefore easily believable, was revealed. I had no knowledge of Satanism and no clue that June had experienced it first-hand. My little bit of research into cults came *after* June disclosed Satanic memories, and I was very careful not to share it with her. I frankly wanted to know if what she told me had been reported by anyone else or had any basis in known fact. If her abuse was just a story, it's not one she got from me.

Can a human being survive such trauma and emerge as a whole and healthy person? Millions of Jews survived the Holocaust and have lived out happy and meaningful lives. June got her kids through college, saved her marriage, and started a new career. She fully integrated her various personalities and no longer dissociates, though she ruefully admits she'd like to at times. She has some occasional anxiety but is able to control it and is no longer depressed or suicidal. Always a devout Christian, her faith has been strengthened by her ordeal many times over. She was even able to forgive her parents and achieve a partial reconciliation with them, a marvelous testimony to her faith, love, and courage.

Multiples are always afraid they'll lose something of themselves in therapy. What really happens is that they find themselves. All of June's "parts" are still there, but now integrated into a coherent, whole person. She's a loving wife and mother, in a very polished and ladylike way ("The '50s Lady"). She's deeply religious and quite moral, but not a prude or fanatic ("Prudence"). She's able to play in a childlike way, but without switching to a child alter ("Little Miss"). And there's an impish note of sarcasm in her humor at times, reminiscent of "The Mocker," but without his venom or spite. Far from being the Devil's daughter, she is truly a child of God.

June's own perspective on her therapy and her memories was revealed at our last session:

"You know, Bob, I've finally realized that I've remembered all this stuff all along; I just couldn't let myself know that I knew." Maybe that's what MPD is really all about.

CHAPTER 13

Multiplicity

PEOPLE WITH MULTIPLE PERSONALITY DISORDER are not several persons residing overcrowdedly in one body. Their various "personalities" are not whole persons but rather are *fragments* of a Self, split off from each other and from the rest of the individual. And because they are isolated pieces they are not well-integrated, fully-developed, three-dimensional persons. Not being tempered and moderated by other aspects of the personality, they tend to be wooden, stereotyped, one-dimensional caricatures: "The Good Mother" or "The Bad Mother," "The '50s Lady" or "Little Miss." These are roles, not persons. This lends an odd quality at times to therapeutic relationships, as if one were interacting with a cartoon character or somebody in a play. It is part of why MPDs tend towards extremities of behavior, with one alter being promiscuous while another is an asexual prude. It is part of why MPD as a life strategy doesn't work very efficiently. It is also the source of some very amusing moments, as we'll see in a bit.

One can easily make a case for the idea that MPD, now officially called "Dissociative Identity Disorder," is not a separate illness at all but simply an extreme variant of Borderline Personality Disorder. Here's the argument:

1. Borderlines and multiples both have a very diffuse sense of identity. They lack a clear idea of who they are and tend to define themselves in relation to others ("George's wife" or "Marty's girlfriend").

2. Both Borderlines and MPDs tend to have difficulties with long-term relationships (although this is less true of many MPDs).
3. Both tend to be impulsive, dramatic, and manipulative with others.
4. Both tend to "split" themselves and others into all-good and all-bad images. They alternate between extremes of idealization and devaluation of both Self and others.
5. Both tend towards impulsive, self-destructive behaviors such as substance abuse, bulimia, sexual promiscuity, and bad driving.
6. Both are prone to self-mutilation and suicidal behavior.
7. Both are emotionally labile.
8. Both tend to feel "empty" inside (because they lack a coherent sense of Self).
9. Both Borderlines and MPDs fear abandonment and react to stress with paranoia and dissociative episodes. They can become frankly psychotic under sufficient stress.

The argument is a compelling one, and it dovetails nicely with the idea that compliant Borderline patients please eager therapists by becoming Multiples on demand. Yet, I've seen MPD patients who did not display classical Borderline personality features. Wanda and June, from Chapter 12, are good examples. Both diagnostic categories are relatively new to psychiatry and are poorly understood at best. The whole concept of a "personality disorder" has developed largely since I started graduate school in 1969. It is worth considering that these diagnostic categories are designed by people, not by Nature, and may or may not reflect anything in the real world. Thus, the names and definitions of personality disorders, as well as other diagnoses, change with each new diagnostic manual, as we grapple with the observation that certain groups of people share some, but not all, personality traits. One can even argue that converting Borderlines into Multiples in therapy is advantageous and appropriate, since MPD can be cured, while BPD is arguably untreatable. Far from constituting malpractice, the iatrogenic conversation of borderline into MPD may represent therapeutic progress!

In any case, multiples perceive themselves as multiple, and it is rude to tell someone, "You're not who you claim to be." So my therapeutic approach is to accept their multiplicity at face value, while remembering that it is a kind of metaphor, not a literal reality. For that matter, if I *did* tell them "MPD is a myth" (which I don't believe) they'd just leave me for a more sympathetic therapist. So I take them at face value and I relate to each alter as he or she presents her- or himself, all the while remembering that I am really dealing with one person and that my goal is to help her reintegrate her subdivided self.

Let me point out again that Multiple Personality Disorder is not the same as Schizophrenia, with which it is often confused. Indeed, the two are no more alike than a bandsaw and a bandicoot. Schizophrenia is a disorder of the brain, almost certainly involving genetic factors, and certainly biological in origin. It can be treated, but not cured, with medications. It may be precipitated by stress, but it is not a post-traumatic or emotional disorder. Its hallmarks are the psychotic symptoms of delusional thinking and hallucinations. MPD, on the other hand, is a psychological reaction to trauma and abuse. Multiples do not have a brain illness and can be treated, even cured, with psychotherapy. They are not psychotic and do not hallucinate, though they do "hear" the "voices" of their alters. One way to tell the difference is to ask where the voices come from. Schizophrenics hear the voices coming from outside their heads, while MPDs typically identify them, correctly, as coming from within their own heads. Schizophrenics are disconnected from reality. Multiples have disconnected the various parts of themselves.

"Barbara" was my second patient with MPD and a remarkable person even without her multiplicity. She was referred by the assistant pastor of her church, a recovering alcoholic and leader of a self-help group for adult children of alcoholics. Barbara was a member of the group and had gotten herself entangled in some very co-dependent relationships with other members. (Dependency is a need to be taken care of by another. Co-dependency is a desperate need to be needed.) Her inability to take care of, or to say no to, these extremely needy women was adding to her already severe depression and producing panic attacks as well.

Barbara was a very successful real estate broker, but she was so afraid to see a therapist that she brought her minister with her. He explained that she would not talk to me directly, but only through him. I was not to question her directly, but instead to pose my inquiries to the minister, who would pass them on to her and relay her answers to me—though we all sat within six feet of each other. It was an awkward and cumbersome procedure and frankly felt a bit artificial, but I played along respectfully, as it was the only way to interview her at all. Barbara was profoundly depressed and was obsessed with suicide. She believed it was immoral to kill herself, but she kept hoping it would just happen. A former bulimic, she was now starving herself and not sleeping, in an effort to enhance the probability of a fatal car accident. She refused to enter a hospital or take medication and denied me access to her husband. He was her high school sweetheart and had himself lost a brother to "suicide by cop," but I could not seek his assistance in keeping Barbara alive. She declined to schedule another appointment.

The next time I saw Barbara she was in the acute care ward of a local psychiatric hospital. She'd been driving around for five days with no food, no water, and no sleep, hoping to get run over by a truck. She was depressed, exhausted, and very nearly psychotic, but she was also impressed that I'd left my wife at a dinner meeting to look in on her. She agreed to accept me as her therapist, no translators required. Her therapy lasted several years and involved numerous hospital stays, dozens of medications, even electro-shock therapy, and more than a few midnight crises and surprises.

Barbara's decompensation (falling apart) had been precipitated by the sex therapy she and her husband had been receiving from another counselor. She'd always loathed sex and seen it as a nasty chore performed only as a duty to her husband. She'd always had vague memories of sexual abuse by her cousin, and these became clearer and more detailed as her counseling progressed. She'd also gotten to the point where she emotionally dissociated or disconnected during sex, putting herself into a kind of trance state where she barely felt what was going on. Now that she was really dealing with her sexuality, her mind was flooded with old memories and shameful, disgusted feelings which worsened each time they made love. And she began to "hear" the voices of other parts of herself, alter egos from her childhood that came out during dissociative episodes. This terrified her. So did the dawning realization that she'd been molested by her uncle as well as her cousin. She arrived at my office again in a nearly psychotic state, and back to the hospital we went.

That's where Barbara's case took on an extra dimension that makes it so memorable to me. Barbara evidenced many of the characteristics of Borderline Personality Disorder, including extreme mood changes, confusion about her identity, chronic feelings of emptiness, fear of abandonment, splitting, and dissociation. But she is very *un*borderline in a key way: she is able to maintain stable, rewarding relationships over long periods of time. She's remained close to her family despite an abusive past, and she and "Kenny" have been married for many years. She has a number of close, loyal friends, including her minister. She connected with me and a psychiatrist without splitting us into good or bad. Now, most surprisingly, she made another new connection.

It happened that Barbara ended up in the hospital at the same time as another of my early MPD patients. Against conventional wisdom and over the protests of the nursing staff, I put the two of them in the same room. It wasn't any stroke of therapeutic genius, just an arrangement I found convenient in visiting them. The results, however, were serendipitous and remarkable. Many therapists are reluctant to put more than one multiple in a therapy group because they tend to compete for attention by becoming wilder, more suicidal, or more self-mutilating. But Barbara and her new roomie never competed. Au contraire, they *helped* each other. If one fell into a panic attack or dissociative state, the other looked after her compassionately, perhaps sitting with her or holding her hand or sharing a stuffed animal. If one was suicidal the other stayed up all night and watched over her. If a new alter came out and revealed information useful to the therapy, the other patient passed it on to me (by their mutual consent). Far from interfering in their management or therapies, the roommate situation provided me with two very helpful junior therapists. Yet they never over-stepped their bounds or interfered with my work. (Again, not what you'd expect from a Borderline.)

To my knowledge this relationship may be unique for MPDs. I have seen other multiples who developed relationships with each other, but they tended to be unstable, self-destructive, even bizarre. For example, I saw a female multiple who was "married" to the male alter of another female multiple. They both swore they were not Lesbians, though I was hard-pressed to discern the difference. They were co-dependent and nearly killed each other competing for suicide of the month honors. Barbara and—we'll call her new friend "Rosalind"—were different. They not only didn't compete, didn't interfere, did provide comfort and support, did inform me of important therapeutic information, and did keep the nurses happy, they also grew to love each other. Despite their differences in age, backgrounds, and lifestyles, Barbara and Rosalind became the best of friends, and in a healthy, non-codependent way. Friendships in the psychiatric hot house typically grow quickly, blossom, and die out just as fast. But not with Rosalind and Barbara. To my knowledge, they're *still* friends, years later. Even more remarkably, their husbands struck up a best-buddy comradeship as well. The four of them have traveled and vacationed and done church work together. These two women, both severely abused and traumatized as children, both split and shattered into multiple selves, both repeatedly hospitalized and medicated, have forged a loyal and loving partnership with each other and their spouses. I have to count that as a genuine human triumph, comparable to the ascent of Mt. Everest.

Barbara's therapy was extremely difficult at times, and she still suffers from a comorbid Bipolar Disorder. Barbara pushed me to the limits at times, the outer edges of my patience, ingenuity, faith, and ability to compromise while remaining firm on matters of principle. I drove her pretty mercilessly at times, forcing her to deal with issues she'd rather repress and bury. Despite my aversion to shock therapy I referred Barbara for ECT. It made her worse and set our therapy back six months. I refused to continue our phone conversation when I heard her working the action of a rifle in the background. Not until I heard the click of a gun cabinet lock would I proceed with this suicide call. (Barbara was and is scrupulously honest and would never fake it. When I heard the cabinet shut, I knew the gun was in it.) When she refused to go home or to the hospital, I allowed her to sleep in her van, parked under the streetlight in front of my house. It wasn't totally safe, but nearly, and it was a violation of my privacy and the separation of my professional and personal lives. But it did keep Barbara alive. Sometimes you have to go beyond the bounds of traditional therapeutic procedures, practices, even ethics, in order to do your job right. Barbara recognized that she'd extended my professional limits and had her grandmother make me a beautiful quilt, which I also went beyond traditional limits to accept.

I also spent a whimsical hour with Rosalind and Barbara together, coloring Easter bunnies in a coloring book, sitting on my office floor. We've all got a child alter hidden in us somewhere. Note, however, that I've not referred to Barbara as "Barb" or "Babs" or, worse yet, "Barbie." These were child alters that had been abused and names I used only in therapeutic reprocessing work. Another alter called herself "Toxic Shame," or "T.S." for short, which referred to her feelings about being sexually molested. (I believe she got this name from a book on survivors of abuse.) This alter was persecutory and drove Barbara to self-mutilation and suicidal acting-out. There were also the "Rebel," stubborn and business-like, but bulimic, "Patsy," a mother/protector alter who sometimes urged her to suicide, and a sexual alter who took over during love-making and relieved Barbara of that little chore. And there was a father alter who criticized and condemned her and drove her both to perfection and to despair.

As an MPD Barbara was not especially complicated, and indeed there was rather little switching of alters, internal communication, and the like. Her alters were not elaborately developed and were really more nearly analogous to different "ego states" or "frames of mind" than to different persons. As a person, though, Barbara is extremely complex, which made her a tremendous therapeutic challenge and a human being whose life has enriched the lives of many, including me.

My most complex case by far was "Dorothy." Maybe the most tragic, too. Dorothy was referred to me as a multiple, though she denied having this problem at first. She'd been in therapy for nearly eight years, first in a psychiatric hospital, then as an outpatient. She was sent to me by the psychiatrist who'd rescued her from twenty-eight years' captivity by her family, then saved her from the Psych residents and nurses who wanted her drugged up or committed, then "adopted" her as his own "foster daughter." This was also going considerably beyond professional limits, but according to Dorothy, he went even further. He sexually molested her, paying particular attention to her Teutonic breasts. Her first "switch" to another personality came in our fourth session. That one was an angry alter I later learned to call "Death." By the third month of therapy Dorothy was regularly switching to "Sarah" and "Linda" and occasionally Death, and there were hints of child alters as well. Sarah was my main contact and access point to an incredible multi-level labyrinth of personalities. By her own count there were over a hundred. Figure 2 represents a partial list provided to me by Sarah. Note that several have the same name but different ages. To Dorothy et al. this made them different persons. "Hurt everybody" refers to abusive alters. Note also the male alters, the abstractions such as "Death" and "Dreamer," and the alters based on real people, such as "Grandpa" and "Good Mother." Much later I was to meet "Martha," an alter I'd never seen or even heard about before. As usual, I introduced myself politely, asked her name and inquired as to her age and function in the personality system. "I get new alters whenever we need one," she replied. I asked how she accomplished this feat. "It's simple; I just go back into this huge room where there's all sorts of different people and pick one that fits the needs of this particular situation. When I bring her out, that's a new alter. Would you like me to get you one now?" I respectfully declined. A hundred personalities seemed quite sufficient to me, and I don't charge by the alter, but by the hour.

Dorothy was a large but not obese woman of Jewish descent. Square-jawed, big-boned, buxom, and tall, she could have been an imposing figure, though not a sensual one. She was bright and articulate and held a nursing degree. Her supervisors rated her professional skills as excellent, though she was very shy and so was formal and distant with both patients and co-workers. Her religion, by the way, was essentially a non-issue, except it probably influenced her doctor (also Jewish) to adopt her. This may be surprising, as she was raised in rural Bible-Belt Alabama, in a lower working class family. The Klan, you'll recall, didn't care for Catholics or Jews much more than they liked "Negroes." But Birmingham has a fairly large, prominent, and well-regarded Jewish community. In my thirty-eight years here I've heard a lot of racial humor and epithets, but rarely an anti-Jewish (or for that matter anti-Catholic) remark.

Our therapy sessions pretty quickly settled into a regular pattern. Dorothy was always punctual, even later on when her back injuries put her temporarily into a wheel chair. I escorted her into the office, dimming the lights in deference to her photophobia, and handing her a stuffed lion to hold. She sat in the same wing-back chair and told me she was more suicidal "right now" than she'd ever been—twice a week for three years. We discussed her current problems and determined what alters were fired up, pissed off, or depressed, and I suggested she switch to Sarah, my MPD travel agent. Sarah filled me in on the status of the System, as best she knew it, then transferred me to the alter du jour to deal with the latest crisis, memory of abuse, suicidal threat, real-world problem, or therapeutic transference difficulty. We'd switch to whatever alters were needed, deal with whatever was pressing, and hopefully switch back to Dorothy by the end of the session. "Dorothy" was often pretty confused at being sent home five minutes after she arrived—by her experience—but she usually took over fairly calmly and drove her selves home. A few times I was left at the end of the hour with a child alter and had to detain her or call for a ride to get her home safely. I can't guarantee I never put a mischievous eight-year-old behind the wheel and sent her unknowingly away for a joy ride.

What gradually emerged in therapy was an unbelievably complex personality structure, which had developed in response to a life of unspeakable horror. No one could function day to day with the memory of the abuse she'd endured, so Dorothy had buried the memories under multiple layers of personae. Year after year she'd created new alters and broken connections to them and others, so that it often required several switches to contact one. Some were hidden so deeply even Sarah, my main guide, didn't know who to talk to to find out who to ask about who might know how to get in touch with the alter who might be aware of "X's" identity. Little by little the alters revealed themselves and Dorothy's horrible and remarkable past.

From her earliest years, Dorothy's family had scapegoated her and singled her out for abuse. Her brother, currently in prison, beat her repeatedly and severely. He shattered her jaws so badly and so often she later required artificial implants and bone grafts to repair and rebuild them. These led to the growth of tumors which have also required medical and surgical interventions. Her brother raped and sodomized her routinely, from toddlerhood on, either by himself or in company with her father and grandfather. One of her child alters described such a gang rape at age six, which left her bleeding and barely able to walk. Her grandmother then administered a caustic douche (probably lye) and enemas to "clean her out" and made Dorothy clean up the bloody mess she made. As she could no longer walk, she did this on her hands and knees. The douches left her permanently sterile. On another occasion her brother "sold" her to a friend for a half-case of beer. The friend tied her to a bed and spent the next forty-eight hours raping and sodomizing her. In her naivete Dorothy had taken a puppy with her for company on this "visit." The brother's friend crushed the puppy's head and smeared its brains over Dorothy's body as he raped her again. She was twelve.

In order to hide Dorothy from the child protection authorities she was kept home from school and rarely allowed out of the house. She was not permitted shoes, as this might have enabled her to run away.

Only as an adult did she manage to overcome her fear and to escape, with the assistance of the mental health center. She got her GED while in the psychiatric hospital.

Therapy with Dorothy was never smooth or easy. The threat of suicide was constant and real, vividly demonstrated by periodic self-mutilation and frequent late-night phone calls. I confiscated a small but impressive collection of knives from her, including the one she used to carve the word "loser" into her thigh. My children came to recognize her and some of her alters and would keep her entertained or distracted until I could get to the phone. She constantly pushed limits, constantly put my loyalty and skills to the test. Therapy was frequently interrupted for her surgical and medical procedures, and I visited her more than once in the hospital. But I never put her in a psychiatric hospital. That she refused. She finally ended up in a wheelchair with what was diagnosed much later as multiple sclerosis. I ultimately came to dread our sessions, never knowing what I'd have to contend with next. Finally she got mad and fired me for "not caring" about her, though I was seeing her twice weekly for little or no fee. I'd refused her a prime five o'clock appointment, and she was offended.

Yet there were also moments of tenderness, beauty, even humor. When Dorothy had to quit work and her insurance lapsed, she gave me several 78 rpm records to play on my Victrola, the only payment she could make. Early in therapy I left the room to get us both a cup of coffee. When I returned, this large woman was sitting cross-legged on the floor, playing with a doll. She looked up shyly and asked in a four-year-old voice who I was. "I'm Missy," she told me. "I'm this many"—holding up four fingers. "Would you play with me?" I had to help her off the floor, since Missy may have been four, but she was in Dorothy's beat-up thirty-year-old body. Another time I met an alter unknown to me, who told me she was "No Name." She was "an evil, disgusting slut" who did not deserve a human name and was rejected by the other personalities. As I got to know her I was impressed by her gentle and caring nature. She was perhaps Dorothy's last effort to create a loving and loveable feminine image for herself. I named her

"Lindy," a name I happen to like and one closely resembling Dorothy's own middle name. She was very grateful.

And then there was "Granny." Dorothy had told me many times about her grandmother's tender home remedies, beatings, and verbal abuse. She was terrified of her Granny, both the real-life one and the alter modeled after her. "Granny" was an abusive alter who mocked Dorothy and the others, criticized and cursed her, and drove her to suicide and self-mutilation. Dorothy had warned me repeatedly how cruel and violent Granny was and emphasized that Granny had a vicious tongue in an extremely foul mouth. Granny, she said, did not like me for befriending her and was especially irate about my Christening of "Lindy." I should be careful if Granny ever came out. I knew of course that Granny existed only in the memory of a scared little girl; she was a part of a person, created by an abused child to protect herself from further pain. Nevertheless, Dorothy had me a bit nervous about meeting this particular alter. Granny had in actual fact caused Dorothy to lacerate herself and take a suicidal overdose on numerous occasions. Would this alter come out in session and attack me? It wasn't beyond possibility. I hadn't heard from Granny yet, but I certainly wasn't going to invite her "out" on my own.

Then in the middle of a pleasant conversation with Sarah, the most helpful and least depressed alter in the System, Dorothy's expression slowly changed until she was glaring hatefully at me. "You sorry-assed, c-sucking, m-f'ing, son of a bitch; I hate your stinking low-life guts," she began, before launching into a stream of really *nasty* curses. "Granny!" I said. "How nice to meet you at last." That stopped her in mid-epithet and nearly put her on the floor. She recovered quickly enough and proceeded to ridicule me for trying to help such a stupid, worthless whore as Dorothy was. Yet I seemed to detect a slight decline in her level of evil enthusiasm. I conceded that Dorothy looked pretty helpless, while also indicating that I intended to do my job the best I could.

Colin Ross says that MPD is "a scared little girl pretending the abuse happened to someone else." Best summary of MPD I've ever heard. Multiples split off parts of their selves to endure the abuse and contain its memory so their central Self can survive. The alters serve a protective function, even the abusive alters. Newcomers to the MPD scene are usually surprised to find the multiple creating alters in the image of her abuser, yet it has a clear logic to it. A protector should be as strong as possible, and who is the most powerful person the abuse victim knows? Her abuser. So I knew that even "Granny" served in some way to protect and preserve the core personality, and I asked her what it was. Granny answered scornfully that she kept Dorothy from doing anything even more stupid than she already had by keeping her ugly (cutting her), criticizing her for trusting others who could abuse her, and generally scaring her from getting too close to anybody. I complimented her on the efficiency with which she performed her role, while noting the danger of killing the patient in order to save her. She seemed to appreciate my flattery and became generally more conversational, so I took a chance and remarked that in some way Granny must actually care about Dorothy, since she took such pains to protect her. And I wondered what kind of incredible abuse Granny herself must have suffered, to make her so mean and cruel. At that her face fell and she quickly switched back to Sarah, but not before I could see that Granny was softly crying. She was, for all her bluff and fury, just a scared little girl after all.

I had no contact with Dorothy for several years after she fired me and I figured she very probably was dead. If the cancer hadn't killed her, she almost surely must have hanged herself. She kept a noose hanging above the trap-door to her attic at all times. Then, in July 2000 she called me from another state. She was working with her foster father in a hospital and had bought a small house there. The tumors in her jaws caused her constant pain and made it difficult for her to talk. She'd been diagnosed with multiple sclerosis and was wheelchair-bound much of the time, as well as in pain from that illness, too. She was more suicidal than she'd ever been "right now" and needed someone to talk to. She turned to me because through it all I was the only person she could trust. We arranged for three telephone therapy sessions, but on each occasion she failed to call. She did leave a message later, saying she was in the hospital, but I never talked to her again. Her check came in the mail, as promised.

Dorothy is her real name, one of only two in this book, used with her permission. She is a woman of great courage, and I admire her greatly.

My funniest, most entertaining multiple would have to be Jennifer. Prettiest, too. Jennifer was slender where a woman is supposed to be and nicely rounded in all the traditional places. With nearly waist-long auburn hair and ivory complexion, she looked like a movie star. She was probably silicone-enhanced, though she never said so, and there was no therapeutically relevant reason to ask. The mother of two, she was bright, well-educated, and a gifted artist. I saw her first at the hospital, where she'd been readmitted for suicidal depression. She'd already been diagnosed MPD, could provide a list of her alters, and switched to another personality in our first or second session. Her therapy started at a fast trot and rarely slowed to much less than a gallop.

There's not much funny about MPD per se, and Jennifer had experienced her fair share of horror and trauma. While her father watched, her mother had thrust candles and small religious statues into her rectum and vagina, exposed her to pornography, thrust her head into vomit, burned her, beat her, and forced her to drink her own urine, all by the age of four or five. At age two her mother purposely placed her on an ant bed, resulting in her hospitalization for hundreds of bites. By the time I saw her, at thirty-two, she'd been raped several times and had been forcibly inducted, she believed, into her mother's Satanic group. No wonder she still slept with a baby blanket, was bulimic, and had several psychiatric hospitalizations in her resume. Here's a brief rundown on her alters and their stories:

1. "Jennifer," age thirty-two. The "host personality," "out" most of the time, married, mother of two (although she had no memory of giving birth to them), employed part-time as a graphic artist.
2. "Bobbie Jo," age thirty-two. First created when Jennifer was five, after being raped and sodomized. A countrified party girl who

loved to drink, fight, flirt, and make kinky love. She had twice been arrested for assault in barroom brawls and claimed to have killed off an alter named "Josie." Had gotten drunk with her nephew, who then forced her to have sex. I called her "The Bad-Ass Bimbo from Bubba-land," but not to her face.

3. "Josie," presumably age thirty-two. A moderately talented artist but now supposedly dead. She resurfaced only once, late in therapy, confirming she was simply hiding out from Bobbie Jo.

4. "Cassandra," also thirty-two. A sweet, simple, and very nurturing "Earth Mother." The System's peace-maker but rarely in evidence.

5. "Josey," age seven and "Josey-O," about four. These were earlier versions of the Josie personality, but maintained semi-independent existence. Josey-O sometimes came out to play with Jennifer's children, much to their delight.

6. "No Name," two years old. Probably the core or original personality, long locked away in fear. She had no name because that would have revealed her presence to abusive alters.

7. "Calvin," presumably also thirty-two. A nice guy, rarely out, whose primary function was to take care of No Name.

8. "Cactus Jack," again thirty-two. A fun-loving cowboy who liked to carouse in honky-tonks and thought Calvin was a "piss-ant fag." The male counterpart of Bobbie Jo, he and B.J. competed for attention and control, but mostly in good humor.

9. "Michelle," an adolescent. A younger, nicer, and tamer version of Bobbie Jo.

10. "Catch Me," about seven. Played games, especially hide-and-seek. No longer had any real function in the system.

11. "Martha," of uncertain age, but definitely older than the other adult alters. An abusive alter, the embodiment of Jennifer's mother. The real-life mother was a witch and a Satanist who tried to force child Jennifer to join a cult and allegedly took her to see the sacrifice of a human baby. "Josie" had tried to dig up the baby later, but her spade pierced the infant's skull, leaving her to feel guilty and ashamed. The other alters all feared and shunned "Martha," who was lonely

and angry at their rejection. I tried to recast her as "Marti," a kind and child-like persona, but the others wouldn't have it. It was Marti who revealed the Satanic ritual and the post-hypnotic suggestion that still kept the Jennifer System enslaved: if she ever told, she and her family would all be killed. Jennifer firmly believed this and avoided all contact with her real mother and father. She claimed they'd vandalized her house, filed false charges on her, and otherwise warned her never to tell. Since she'd told me, my name would be added to the hit list, so I was happy to pledge my complete silence, until now.

Jennifer was one of my Borderline MPDs, and there was plenty of therapeutic uproar. She'd miss an appointment, then call in suicidal and needing hospitalization. The drama surrounding the revelation of Martha's Satanism was worthy of a night-time soap opera. Still, a lot of the work was fun. The child alters were playful; Cassandra was sweet; and Jennifer was intelligent and committed to her therapy. Cactus Jack liked to stop by and shoot the bull with me, while B.J. flirted with me harmlessly but outrageously. That's what led to the most comical single moment of my MPD career:

It was usually Jennifer who came into the session "out," i.e., conscious. She would be modest and demure and polite, not hiding her figure, but not flaunting it either. But on this occasion she came strutting down the hall in six-inch pumps and a low-cut, no-back mini-dress that was skin-tight and about one molecule thick. She was all legs and breasts, hips driving and eyes shining with the promise of passion fulfilled. This was clearly not "Jennifer."

"Hey, Bobbie Jo; how ya doing?" I asked.

"Oh, pooh," she grinned. "How did you know it was me?" "My astute clinical intuition," I thought, but I kept it to myself.

Bobbie Jo sat down and crossed her legs, revealing another three inches of thigh. She played seduction games for a while, asking if I liked her dress, teasing me for being a prude, and suggesting various scenarios we might enact. She was sexy, yet playful, knowing I'd enjoy the show but wouldn't accept her offers or her challenges. Eventually she seemed to get tired or maybe just bored, and her eyes went blank.

Suddenly she perked up and lounged back, crossed her legs man-style (revealing anything else she'd covered up so far) and said in a surprisingly masculine voice, "Hey, Doc, how they hanging, Old Hoss?" It was Cactus Jack, out for a surprise visit. Then he looked down at him-(her?) self, bolted upright in disgust and shouted, "Shiiit! Dammit, I told that bitch not to go out dressed this way. It's goddamned embarrassing to be seen like this." Poor old Jack tried to stretch the skirt down over his slender legs, but only succeeded in exposing more voluptuous bosom. He pulled it back up, to keep anything from falling out, but looked like a showgirl again down below. He fought that dress top and bottom, but the laws of physics were against him. It was an amazing sight, and I couldn't entirely suppress a snicker and a snort. Fortunately Cassandra took over and saved Jack from terminal embarrassment. Once again, MPD had shown itself to be a singularly inefficient way to organize a personality.

Why is "multiplicity" a topic of such fascination to so many of us? Perhaps it's because multiples offer a unique perspective on what it means to be a person. What do I really mean when I refer to my "self?" Multiples seem bizarre and exotic with their myriad of selves, yet aren't we all many persons in one? I'm a son, a brother, a husband, a father, a psychologist, a teacher, and a writer. I'm also a bicyclist, a Bonsai artist, a gardener, a lover, a sinner, and (rarely) a saint. In each of these roles I'm a somewhat different person, and my feelings and behaviors are different. Yet I'm also aware that all of these are *me*. Certainly, I am not the same person I was at ten or twenty or even forty. Do I act the same way with the preacher as I do in bed with my wife? What about in bed with the preacher's wife? Yet, I have a sense of essential Me-ness. I can recognize myself in my memories of the past and across a wide range of situations. An MPD has lost that awareness, that sense of a continuous core

Self, but she also is truly only one person, subdivided into various roles and self-images. We tend to think of our own consciousness as a unitary phenomenon, yet a guitarist can strum with one hand, work the fret board with the other, tap his foot, sing a song, and watch for audience reaction, all at the same time. Isn't each activity directed by a separate center of consciousness? We've already seen that dissociation is a universal experience, and Freud taught us that unconscious thought processes occur in all of us. Are multiples really so different, then?

What does seem quite different about MPDs is that they have suffered trauma and abuse far worse than most of us ever experience or even dream of. Lara's father sodomized her with an ice pick and stuffed live creatures into her vagina, to die there and rot. Dorothy was raped and beaten by all her family and her reproductive tract destroyed by her grandmother's "cleaning solution." June and Jennifer were tortured and molested by Satanic groups, and June was forced into cannibalism and vampirism. If Hitler's Holocaust or bin Laden's terrorism weren't convincing enough, these and other patients with MPD provide ample evidence that no act is so hideous, brutal, or "inhuman" that some human doesn't do it to another every day.

Yet, for all of this, these women survived their Hellish childhoods and endured. They were left fragmented and scarred, depressed and suicidal, but they endured. Amazingly, most of them also found ways to be happy. They found remarkably supportive husbands, started careers, raised children. They ended up being nice people. If MPD reveals to us the very worst of humanity, it also provides a glimpse at some of the best. That's why my MPD stories are some of my very favorite "Psycho-stories." MPD shows us the incredible range of the human psyche, which is what attracted me to this business in the first place. By the way, most of the patients in this book are identified by pseudonyms, in order to protect their true identities. But "Dorothy" is truly Dorothy, called here by her true name, by her own request. I guess she's just too tired of living out the lives of aliases, not to mention just too fundamentally honest, to go by some other name in this account of her life. She is a remarkable and admirable woman who requires enormous courage just to face each new day. I can only hope that telling her story will provide some measure of consolation for her, perhaps knowing that her life will inspire other victims of abuse to recapture their identities and the meaningfulness of their existence.

CHAPTER 14

Junkies and Juicers

I'M REALLY NOT VERY FOND of working with addicts. I try to be sympathetic, because addicted people are truly in pain. Granted, their pain
is self-induced, but then isn't most pain caused by our own doings
or lifestyle? But addicts tend to be self-absorbed, self-destructive,
and self-defeating. They are typically manipulative, dependent, and
deceitful. They even lie to themselves; it's called "denial." I find them
tedious and try to avoid them as patients. This is impossible, however,
especially if you see families, as I do. My depressed women patients
are married to alcoholics who take advantage of them and abuse their
ADHD kids. In despair the wives turn to Xanax or smoke their teenagers' dope. Substance abuse is so pervasive it's unavoidable, even to a
mostly child/adolescent psychologist.

Not that there haven't been a few memorable or even enjoyable
druggies in my career. There was, for example, the not-too-bright nineteen-year-old who had the good fortune to find a rich girlfriend. She'd
scored a quarter million off her husband's insurance when he'd driven
off a bridge in a drunken stupor. He was a high school dropout and was
only occasionally and minimally employed. Suddenly he had vast sums
at his disposal. In three months he wrecked two new cars and blew
$60,000 on crack cocaine. This mindless and lazy person will never
again in his life see 60k in cash money. Here was a college education, a
new house, start-up capital for his own business, a sure-fire retirement

package. He sent it all up in smoke. He also fried so many neurons he couldn't even remember all the fun he'd had. Another crack-head came to the hospital with all his possessions on his body. He'd lost his savings, his job, his reputation, his wife and kids, his car, house and all his possessions, his freedom and his self-respect. All to cocaine. We kept him clean and sober for twenty-eight days, then discharged him. He walked two blocks directly to the nearest crack house. Nicotine is the most addictive substance known (with the possible exception of Taco Flavored Doritos, now long since off the market) but cocaine's a close second. I've seen crack-heads who burglarized their own parents and sold their own babies to buy coke.

The problem with getting high is that eventually you have to get low again, and that feels awful. You can put off the inevitable by doing more drugs, but sooner or later you run out or give out and then you crash. A young couple I saw in Austin ran "speed" for nearly a week, then ran out. They felt so awful they trashed their apartment, then beat each other up. And they were in love. Withdrawal from Xanax (prescribed by her doctor) put one of my MPD patients in the hospital for a month. The worst withdrawal I've seen was a VA patient who'd been averaging a quart and a half of gin nightly for twenty years, and cheap gin at that. He got locked up a couple of days and went into "DT's." Delirium tremens often causes a hallucinatory sensation like bugs crawling about under your skin. ("That makes my skin crawl," as the saying goes.) To this old soldier it seemed as if a little man was scrambling about inside him, struggling to get out. So he took a hatchet and chopped off three toes as an escape route. Apparently it worked, but the little man wasn't real, while the toes were.

Falling off the wagon can be worse than getting on, especially if there are complicating factors. I treated a recovering alcoholic who took Prozac for the depression he experienced when booze and his wife abandoned him. He was doing better and was cautioned not to drink, but he couldn't resist one more night on the town. He got ripped, and the alcohol combined with the medication brought out the angry sociopath within. He beat up his wife and did ninety days in the city jail. He never came back to see me, which was fine, but he also never paid my bill.

Anything that gives you a buzz, cranks up your endorphins, makes you feel good, is potentially addictive. Some pleasure-seeking is okay, even if it's pretty obsessive. My Bonsai buddies and I are pretty fanatical about our trees, for example, and the art itself demands an obsessive-compulsive, almost addictive approach. Miss a day's watering and you've got a dead tree. But there's no crash, no hang-over, no mad cravings—well, maybe for a really great Satsuki azalea. What makes something addictive is that the very thing which makes you feel great now makes you feel lousy later. The hang-over is as much a part of the alcohol binge as is the euphoria that precedes it. Dirty pictures arouse you, then leave you disgusted with yourself. Addicts haven't learned a fundamental secret to happiness in life: there's no free lunch. You pay for your goodies, one way or another. When you buy now and pay for it later, you pay with interest, and a short-term pay-off almost inevitably entails a long-term loss. Likewise, a short-term investment of time, energy, or money typically yields a long-term reward. A college degree takes four years of hard work, thousands of hours in labs and libraries, and many thousands more in tuition payments (increasingly in the form of student loans). But recent research shows that a four-year college degree vastly increases earning potential, raises your social status, and gets you a much more interesting job—for the rest of your life. The smart money always looks to the long run, which is when the big payoffs and the big losses are generally to be found. The addict gratifies his impulses now and pays through the nose later, if he even *has* a later—or a nose.

Junkies will do most anything to get high, even if it's embarrassing, expensive, or dangerous. At the PACE program we had an adolescent who'd sniff anything he could get his hands on. We couldn't keep felt-tip pens, for example, because "Timothy" would drop them in a bag and snort the fumes. If you could get high on excrement, Timothy's head would be in the toilet. Just for fun, we told him the ultimate high was on Elmer's Glue. He promptly stole a bottle from the staff office and came reeling out of his room with white goop dripping off his face. There is, of course, nothing in Elmer's that will intoxicate you; it's completely safe. But that didn't stop Timothy. He was as knee-walking drunk as anybody I've ever seen. A lot of the high is just "in your head" anyway, even with a truly intoxicating substance. In Austin, my Chicano patients hotly debated the relative merits of black versus silver spray paint, though the solvent and propellant were identical.

It's hard enough for any adolescent to fit in and be considered "cool," but it's much harder for the hearing-impaired. They are different and to adolescents different is bad (unless it's the "right" kind of different, which is to say whatever particular form of deviance or rebellion is currently in vogue). Deaf kids also miss out on a lot because they can't hear. A surprising amount of learning is incidental: over-heard conversations, background music, non-captioned TV. The hearing-impaired miss all this and thus find it harder to stay in the loop. So they have to try harder to be cool. An easy way for any teen to gain acceptance is to become a druggie. The admission requirements for this group are extremely simple. You just do dope. A deaf patient of mine struggled desperately to fit in and be liked, and he resorted to this drug strategy. Fortunately, his mom found his stash of pills and brought them, and him, to me. A few of them I recognized as minor tranquilizers or pain pills, both of which have abuse potential. I found another couple in the PDR (*Physicians' Desk Reference*, a book listing all prescription medicines) and some were over-the-counter sinus tablets, not dangerous unless mixed with alcohol. But several of the pills stumped me. The pharmacist at the mental health center identified an older barbiturate and some other pain pills, but the others left him as baffled as I was. He took them to Samford University's school of pharmacy, where he was on the faculty, and consulted his colleagues and the school library. He found the pills in a book of veterinary medicines.

Returning the pills to my patient's mother, I discussed with her son the results of my investigation. They were mixed, I said. "The bad news is, you won't get high on this stuff. The good news is, you won't get worms, either."

Honesty is the most fundamental requirement for psychotherapy, and it is often lacking in substance abusers. That's one reason I routinely refer my patients to AA and NA. Other recovering addicts know the score first-hand and see through denial and flat-out deceit a lot better than I can. But I also feel hypocritical working with addicts, partly due to the utter irrationality of U.S. drug laws. I drink alcohol, as does almost everyone I know. I used to smoke a pipe and still could if I wanted to (though my wife says not in the house.) But nicotine kills far more people than *all* other drugs combined; alcohol is a distant second. And they are both legal. Marijuana is illegal, though on a list of killer drugs it wouldn't make the top fifty. How do I explain to a teenaged pot-smoker why it's okay to use my drug of choice, but not okay to use his, especially when mine causes addiction and cirrhosis, and his is not only benign, but has proven medical benefits? Besides, while I haven't smoked pot in many years, back in the '70s everybody I knew smoked dope. The best I ever had, legendary "Panama Red," was at a professor's house. So how can I honestly tell my patient to knock it off? Adolescents are acutely sensitive to hypocrisy, irrationality, and unfairness in authority figures. Our drug laws are riddled with these qualities, making therapy with young drug offenders a troubling experience.

Working with addicts can get pretty bizarre, even grotesque at times. Dr. James Barnett and I worked with a coke addict at Hill Crest, a case that took a weird and nearly deadly turn. The man was admitted for cocaine addiction, but it was quickly evident that he was clinically depressed as well. Dr. Barnett gave him a mild tranquilizer to help him sleep and put him on a standard anti-depressant such as Zoloft. Off of his self-medication and on the proper drug, the man recovered rapidly. His intelligence, wit, and compassion for others were gratifying to see, and he quickly became a favorite of patients and staff alike. Meanwhile, my psychological evaluation revealed that he suffered from ADHD as well. This was not surprising, as ADHD is strongly associated with both depression and substance abuse. We found ourselves in something of a dilemma, however, as this fellow was in the hospital for cocaine abuse, and cocaine is a stimulant, just as the medication for

ADHD—Ritalin, Dexedrine, Adderall, etc.—is a stimulant. In fact, they are chemical first cousins. Do we prescribe an abusable drug to a known abuser, or do we deprive him of the treatment of choice for a demonstrated disorder? Cautiously, we put him on Ritalin, carefully dosing him and closely monitoring the results. He did great. He was much calmer, more organized, and less impulsive. Again his improvement was gratifying and dramatic.

So we sent him home, still on his anti-depressant and, with some trepidation on our parts, still on Ritalin. He immediately ground up the Ritalin, loaded it into a syringe and shoved it into his arm. It could have killed him, and it surely killed our enthusiasm for treating comorbid addiction and ADHD.

Alcoholism is a tricky, complicated business, which is one reason I like to leave it to the pros or, better yet, to the talented amateurs of AA. It's not even easy to define, as it doesn't depend solely on frequency or quantity. There are daily drinkers who aren't alcoholics. In fact, doctors tell us a glass or two of wine every day is probably good for your cardiovascular system. Contrariwise, one of the most severe cases I ever ran across was a Chinese immigrant named "Taiwan Ahn," who drank only once a year and was absolutely cold sober the rest of the time. Come Christmas Eve he'd check into a hotel with all the Irish Whisky he could carry and drink until he passed out. When he awoke, he'd drink until he passed out. He repeated this cycle until he got busted or dumped into a hospital, which usually took two to three weeks. Eventually he died of acute alcohol poisoning.

Alcoholism also complicates therapy, especially marital therapy. It's like an ever-present Silent Partner in the couple's interactions and in the therapy. "Hell, Baby, I didn't mean that; it was the beer talking." "I must have forgotten I promised to do that. Guess I had a little too much to drink." "I know I got really mad, but you shouldn't mess with me when I'm drinking." "I was not drunk; I only had a couple of beers." You never know if the problem is a marital relationship issue, a bit of personal psychopathology, or just a drinking problem. So you go round and round and get nowhere in therapy until you eliminate the substance abuse. Alcoholism and other substance abuse is always treated first. Anything else is a waste of time.

I don't want to seem too negative or judgmental here. Anybody can become addicted to alcohol or other drugs, especially if there's a genetic predisposition in the family. Many alcoholics are exceptionally sensitive and creative human beings. That may be one reason they drink, to dull the pain of seeing human life as it is. Many recovering addicts are embued with a contagious enthusiasm for life and a dedication to honesty, responsibility, and personal involvement with others that is truly inspiring. My own first recovering alcoholic was Winnie M., the wife of one of my professors. I was visiting in their home one evening when she excused herself to go to an AA meeting. I was surprised. "I didn't know you were an alcoholic. How long has it been since your last drink?" I asked.

"Forty years," she said. "I know it's a long time to go to meetings, but it's worked so far, and I can't afford to take any chances. Besides, these people are my family, my community, the finest people I know."

"Have a nice time," was all I could muster in reply.

Addiction is a terrible illness. I wish we'd start treating it as one and rehabilitating instead of incarcerating its sufferers. I admire both the people who treat it and the people who recover from it. All the same, I prefer to invest my professional energies in other directions. Make mine a good old Borderline or an encopretic toddler or maybe just another outrageous adolescent. Give me a nice married couple who are cheating on each other, a marriage on the rocks, if you like, shaken, not stirred, please.

CHAPTER 15

Body and Soul

FREUD'S BIG INTEREST WAS IN "hysteria." It was quite a fashionable illness at the time and fit beautifully into his Psychoanalytic theory. The original idea (going back to ancient Greece) was that women who had never conceived a child had a "barren womb" that was somehow distressed over this situation. ("Hyster" is the old Latin term for the uterus or womb. Think "hysterectomy.") The uterus, then, ran amok through the body, producing all sorts of emotional and physical symptoms. And only in women, of course. Women got all anxious, distressed, and depressed. And, most dramatically, they developed physical symptoms or illness for which there was no demonstrable medical cause or explanation. They went blind. Deaf. They were paralyzed. Freud saw many such patients and he devised a theory to explain them and a therapy to treat them.

Their illness, he said, was the result of the forced forgetting, or "repression," of sexual desires which brought one's self into conflict with the demands of society or of one's own conscience. Perhaps one had been severely punished as a child for masturbating. The desire to do so would then be threatening and would raise one's anxiety level, a very uncomfortable feeling. The solution is repression: simply push the forbidden impulse into one's unconscious mind and remain blithely unaware of it. Trouble is, the energy invested in this forbidden sexual impulse had to go somewhere, and it sort of popped out in the formation of hysterical, often physical, symptoms. This resolved the internal conflict over these impulses, and thereby solved the problem, though at the expense of an hysterical neurosis. The whole process is unconscious, so the patient does not know whence her symptoms derive. It is the analyst's job to help figure this out and make the unconscious connections available to the patient's awareness. This will resolve the crisis and cure the patient.

Freud's thinking was really quite radical for his day. This was back in psychology's infancy, when phrenologists were assessing patients' personality by the sizes of the bumps on their heads, and Freud's colleague, the charlatan Anton Mesmer, was treating mental patients with what he swore was "animal magnetism." (Hence, our word "mesmerizing.") The idea that physical disease could be caused by a mental disorder was unheard of, much less the notion it could be treated by merely talking with the patient. The general public knew next to nothing about Psychology or how to think in psychological terms. Freud changed all that.

Today the situation is very different. Freudian thought and psychological thinking in general have become part of our culture. Everybody knows about the Unconscious, about Repression, about the Oedipus Complex and a host of other psychoanalytic terms. The "Couch" in this book's title refers to the couch Freud used in his consulting room. As I walked across the UAB campus this morning, I overheard a student telling her friend about another friend who is "so anal-retentive," another Freudian concept that has entered the popular jargon. But the development of hysteria requires that the whole process operate at an unconscious level. Repression won't lead to symptom formation if you know you're doing it. The result is that hysteria has all but disappeared. If somebody suddenly goes blind for no reason, everybody knows it is "all in their head." "Hysteria" isn't even a formal diagnostic term any more, having been replaced by "Factitious Disorder" (partly because "hysteria" is politically incorrect, a term which is denigrating to women.) So, in thirty-six years of practice, I've seen only two really classic cases, both in rural Southern women who were too unsophisticated to know better.

The first, actually, was little more than a child, a thirteen-year-old from a small farming town in central Alabama. She had quite suddenly gone totally blind, for no apparent reason. After extensive medical tests, her doctors assured us there was no physiological reason for her blindness. Tests showed conclusively that she could in fact see normally. Dr. Barnett and I admitted her to the Adolescent Psychiatry Unit at Birmingham's Brookwood Hospital.

"Nora" fit in quite nicely and was a very pleasant, cooperative, even cheerful patient. In fact, that was our first clue as to the nature of her disorder. When one goes suddenly blind, at age thirteen, one ought to be terrified and in great distress. Nora's parents certainly were. But Nora seemed blithely unconcerned. This is a common finding in hysteria, also called a "conversion reaction." It is called "la belle indifference," a beatific lack of concern about one's illness. Not that Nora was in any way consciously faking, which is formally called "malingering," and which often betrays itself by overly dramatic emotionality. Yet, it was as if some part of Nora's mind knew all along she was physically okay, just as Freud had explained. We also noticed that Nora had no trouble negotiating her way around the hallways, eating, or other activities she was suddenly forced to do without the aid of her vision. And if you thrust your hand towards her face, Nora flinched, though just a little bit. Clearly she could see. So why was she "blind?"

Carl Jung, one of Freud's disciples, noted that often a neurosis, including hysteria, may by the nature of its symptomatology point to the cause of the problem. A morbid fear of being bitten by rats, for example, might betray an underlying oral aggressiveness that has been repressed and projected onto the rodents. So maybe there was something Nora wanted very much not to see. And in fact, there was. It turned out that Nora had seen her father with his mistress, a discovery she very much wanted not to have made. Her blindness was a way of not seeing Dad's affair, not to mention a terrific way to distract the whole family from the marital situation and to curtail Dad's opportunities for romantic liaisons. Freud would probably also interpret her blindness as a result of her own repressed sexual desires for her father, stirred up in Nora by her awareness of his sexual acting-out. Remember the Oedipus/Electra Complex? In any case, some marital and family counseling helped Nora to regain her vision, and Mom to regain her husband. Dad's lover was on her own. Oddly, at one point in her hospitalization Nora also developed a partial paralysis in one leg. We never did figure that one out, but it resolved spontaneously. Maybe it was Nora's way to keep herself from kicking Dad's butt, or perhaps kicking him out altogether.

My other true hysteric was Shaquita, a near thirty-ish black lady who grew up in an even smaller town near Birmingham. She was living proof that it is possible to have a college degree and remain utterly unaware of the functioning of the world (if such proof be needed). Shaquita was living with her mother, having graduated, then taken an art-related job in Los Angeles California and failed miserably. Not surprising, since she had no artistic ability or knowledge. (She was an Art History major.) She alleged that she was harassed, even sexually assaulted by her boss, an older man with whom she had a quasi-romantic relationship. She was herself nearly arrested in the subway for shoving a man she believed to be stalking her. Returning to Alabama, she still believed he was aware of her thoughts and actions, though there was no evidence he'd left LA. She had no friends and was unemployed, having failed at a customer service job in Birmingham. She was depressed and was increasingly isolating herself from her family. She'd go with Mother to visit relatives, but then she'd sit alone in the kitchen, refusing to socialize and muttering to herself. Most peculiarly, her plan was to attend medical school, either Harvard or Johns Hopkins, although she had never studied biology or chemistry and hadn't applied to either school. At nearly thirty, with a college degree, she thought she could simply show up at the school of her choice, give them the tuition money, and be admitted. Now that's naive!

It was at the customer service job that her conversion reaction or hysteria appeared: she developed a profound stutter, which obviously prevented her from talking to the customers. She was sent to me for a diagnostic consultation by Dr. Barnett, who was treating her for depression. He wanted to know what I thought of her speech problem—did it have a psychological basis? Was she psychotic? Did she have an intelligence problem? So, I gave her part of an IQ test, on which she scored at the Average level, and the Minnesota Multiphasic Personality Inventory (MMPI), which came back questionably valid and indicating all sorts of psychopathology, but probably not an acute psychosis. I am not a speech pathologist, but I did notice a couple of odd things about Shaquita's "stutter." First, stuttering begins in childhood. I've never heard of anyone developing this problem as an adult, at least not in the absence of known brain injury or disease, of which she had neither. So the timing and the presentation suggested a psychological, not a language or neurological, problem. Second, there was an odd quality to her stutter. She didn't repeatedly stumble over the first phoneme (sound; letter) of a word, but instead doggedly repeated the whole syllable. For example, if I asked her to say, "Batman," she wouldn't go, "Buh . . . buh . . . buh . . . ", etc. Instead, she'd say, "Bat . . . bat . . . bat," i.e., three phonemes. This didn't seem right. She'd also keep on trying to say the word when it was obvious that she knew I understood what she was trying to say. I tried to get her to substitute "Caped Crusader" or "The Dark Knight," but that was a no-go, too. My conclusion was that this was an hysterical speech impairment, although I'd never heard of one before.

Shaquita was a diagnostic puzzle. She could have had an unknown neurological condition causing her stutter, but there was no evidence to support this theory. She could have been faking it, that is, "malingering." I've seen plenty of malingerers, mostly people trying to do poorly on IQ tests to get their "dumb dollars" from Social Security Disability. Ironically, kids who do this almost always trip themselves up because they are poorly coached by their none-too-bright parents and too dumb themselves to fake it consistently. For example, on the Vocabulary section they'll define a cow as "a four-legged farm animal you ride on." They obviously know what a cow is and are purposely giving a wrong answer. I used to love to catch them at it. But I didn't think Shaquita was malingering, mostly because I didn't think she was sophisticated enough to come up with the idea.

As to the rest of her symptoms, her social isolation, mumbling to herself, and paranoia, all suggested a psychotic process such as schizophrenia. But she reported no hallucinations, and her ideas were peculiar but not clearly delusional, and these are the two major symptoms of schizophrenia. And there was no family history of the disorder. Shaquita didn't seem "truly crazy," just "merely weird." She could carry on a coherent conversation, but it would be distinctly odd. She was eccentric and she preferred to be alone, and she had no interest in romantic relationships. And all of that pointed to the other diagnosis I gave her. I believe she suffered from a Schizotypal Personality Disorder.

As I've outlined in this book, "personality disorders" are patterns of abnormal thought, emotion, and behavior that are so pervasive over time and different situations as to constitute a permanent (or nearly so) part of one's personality. Schizotypal personalities possess the following characteristics:

1. Acute discomfort with and reduced capacity for close relationships
2. Odd beliefs or magical thinking, e.g., belief in clairvoyance or that others are somehow aware of one at a distance
3. Unusual perceptual experiences
4. Odd thought and speech
5. Suspicious or paranoid ideation
6. Inappropriate or constricted affect
7. Odd, eccentric behavior
8. Lack of close friends

These are taken from the *Diagnostics and Statistical Manual of the American Psychiatric Association*. Sadly, they fit our girl all too well. More sadly, many schizotypals progress to a true schizophrenic illness. The personality disorder might be considered the "prodromal" or leading-up-to phase of schizophrenia. I sent Shaquita back to Dr. Barnett, but followed her case through him. Regrettably, she did progress to a florid psychotic break, requiring hospitalization and confirming my diagnosis of Schizotypal Personality Disorder. A shame, especially because I think she was a nice, if stubborn, kid.

I suppose it's a sign of progress that we've become so psychologically sophisticated that "hysteria" barely exists anymore. But I can't help feeling a bit nostalgic for the old days, when a sweet, mildly retarded young woman was referred to me for a seizure disorder. I asked her to show me a "seizure," and she cooperatively removed her glasses, folded her hands as in prayer, and lay gently on the ground, her head resting comfortably on her hands. It was her way of controlling her mom, but not done consciously. Hey, my third case! And if poor Freud were around today, he'd have to practice in Timbuktu. Or has the Internet hit there too? Meanwhile, I'm left with a mighty short chapter here.

CHAPTER 16

Dr. Bob's Couch

MY WORK AS A PSYCHOLOGIST has exposed me to a wide range of passions and professions, but especially to medicine and the law. My medical exposure was heaviest during my tenure at the Medical Center East Family Practice Residency Program, where I was the behavioral health professor. I am not formally trained in medicine and even managed to dodge the study of chemistry and biology in college. Yet I am called upon to make recommendations about medications, differentially diagnose physical from psychological disorders, and at least understand the emotional, behavioral, and physical symptoms of a large number of different diseases. Psychologists actually treat patients for many basically "physical" or "medical" disorders, including anorexia and bulimia, chronic pain, enuresis and encopresis, headaches, irritable bowel syndrome, and many others. We also try to help people cope with all sorts of other illnesses, from heart attack and stroke to cancer or multiple sclerosis. It's a good thing I read a lot.

I enjoy this aspect of my work; maybe I should have been a "real" doctor. But then, physicians want to play shrink, trumpet players all want to sing, and lawyers and preachers want to switch from pulpit to courtroom and back. Everybody wants the other guy's job, it seems. I've also learned all sorts of little tricks for dealing with medical conditions which often don't respond to drugs or other classically medical interventions. Thus, relaxation training and cognitive therapy can outperform tranquilizers in the treatment of panic disorder, and reverse psychology can succeed with encopretics where mineral oils and laxatives have failed. The classic treatment for thumb-sucking is to paint the offending digit with a Tabasco-like pepper sauce. They tried this on my sister as a child, but she didn't quit the habit until she wanted to. What she did do was develop a life-long craving for Mexican food. What will cure thumb-sucking and other nervous habits is to reward the non-occurrence of the behavior. Attending to it, even with punishment (hot pepper sauce) often exacerbates the problem because it makes the child more anxious. It also gives him a powerful way to rebel. Instead, give attention for doing something else, and she'll likely drop the habit on her own.

One of the oddest of these little medical problems I've been called upon to treat is formally called "urinary retention" or "inhibited micturition," but is more popularly known as "Bashful Bladder Syndrome." It consists of an inability to pee in public places. It sounds trivial, even silly, but there's a fairly extensive medical literature on this disorder, and for good reason. It can be an unexpectedly disabling problem because its sufferers must greatly limit their time away from home, never exceeding the capacity of their bladder. It can require emergency catheterization to empty the bladder or even repeated self-catheterization, with its risk of injury or infection. It can even lead to renal failure, as urinary pressure builds up and backs up the tubes from the kidneys. Less seriously, but still tragically, I saw a woman whose bashful bladder prevented her from taking a free six-week trip to Scotland and Wales. We hadn't sufficient time to treat her, and she couldn't handle the thought of public restrooms, European-style shared hotel facilities, lavatories in trains and airplanes, not to mention countless hours with a painfully distended bladder. Maybe, if I could have gone *with* her . . .

Bashful bladder syndrome is also embarrassing, in fact surprisingly so. This is especially the case for men, whose masculinity is in doubt if they can't "make big water." Ask any guy who's stood at the trough in a stadium men's room, with a long line of beer-drinking fans lined up behind him to pee, and he can't get the flow started. In my thirty-plus years of clinical practice, the only patient who insisted on using an alias to protect his confidentiality, even from me, was a man who couldn't pee in a public pot. I told him the average latency between unzipping and starting the flow of urine was about ten seconds, with twenty seconds still quite within the normal range. That was our goal, and the technique I suggested was to distract himself from thoughts of failure by counting backwards from twenty to one. It worked well and he left a happy, empty, and still anonymous man.

The practice of psychotherapy also tends to involve one with the legal profession, which is often less enjoyable than the medical exposure. Being the son of a law professor, I grew up arguing with an attorney, so I'm not much intimidated by their courtroom shenanigans. I know enough about how the law works, or doesn't work, to hold my own on the witness stand and testify in my own words. Still, there's something pretty scary about the judge in his black robe, the oaken-paneled courtroom and a guy getting $200 an hour to make you look foolish. I've not developed much of a forensic practice because it disrupts my clinical work with last-minute court calls, because the legal maneuvering annoys me, because it involves you with a lot of sleazy people (some of the lawyers and all the crooks) and because the adversarial process is so antithetical to the way psychotherapists think. But as a psychologist I end up at least on the fringes of the legal system, like it or not. I wound up seeing a Ford Explorer case, for example, because they needed a therapist as well as a professional witness. Alabama has been under court order for over two decades to provide appropriate services for children in the foster care system, the result of a child named "R.C." who sued the state on behalf of all foster kids. R.C. was left to rot in psychiatric hospitals for over two years because the Department of Human Resources had nowhere else to put him. I'm not the guy who kept him in the hospital for two years, but I am the guy who first put him there. He needed it, too, coming from an abusive and neglectful home.

In some ways lawyers and psychologists are working the same side of the street. We both deal with humans at their worst, seeing the private decay beneath the glittering public facade. We're both trying to help people get what they need and recover from others' mistreatment. We both see a great variety of people in uniquely complex circumstances and intricate interrelationships. Investigation and analysis, as well as negotiation and persuasion, constitute major aspects of our work. We both make our living working mostly with unhappy clients. (Come to think of it, a lot of this applies to medicine as well, and maybe the ministry too.) But there are major differences in our approaches, too.

Our legal system is based on an adversarial model. There's a plaintiff or a prosecutor versus a defendant. It's me against you, winner takes all, and loser pays the attorneys, goes to jail, loses custody, etc. The goal is to sort out the good guys from the bad guys, and no one wears a gray hat. This isn't an unreasonable approach, but it runs directly opposite to the philosophy and practice of psychotherapy, especially marriage and family work. Here the goal is to find a solution in which everybody wins. Every effort is made to avoid labeling anybody as bad, to understand people's motives and interpret their behavior as positively as possible. Cooperation and compromise are valued; criticism and conflict are discouraged. Everybody wears an off-white hat with a few smudges on it, and occasionally a pretty feather.

Many therapists experience a kind of culture shock when compelled to give expert testimony. They are asked to provide scientifically validated "truth," when all they have is a clinical "impression." They are pressed for yes or no answers when they want to respond "sometimes" or "it depends" or "they tend to." They are required to take sides affirmatively when they see justice in both sides' positions. Most of my own courtroom testimony has been in child custody cases, where I usually don't think either one of them is a fit parent. No doubt lawyers find us therapists as frustrating to question as we find their interrogatories at odds with our own views of human reality.

For all that, I have had some interesting times in court and made some good friends in the legal community. I once saw a judge hold a mother in contempt of court for denying visitation to her child's father. The father was so emotionally abusive the boy vomited and got diarrhea every time he visited. He was losing so much weight the pediatrician was concerned and had advised against further contact. So had I, as the effect on the child's emotional health was just as damaging. But the judge was miffed at his decree being ignored. He gave the child to his father and put the mother in jail for a week. This judge was a nice man, who helped with the church choir and shared a piece of coconut cream pie with me in his chambers. He also was hot-tempered and a bit too impressed with his own power and authority.

More recently, I was called upon to testify in a murder trial, my first, but regretfully not my last. It was held in a small town in a rural Alabama county I'd never visited before, and my first problem was finding the courthouse. Uncharacteristically, it was not downtown on the Square. That was the *old* courthouse. I couldn't understand the tobacco-chewing old farmer who gave me directions to the new one, so I arrived a little late. All I was intended to testify to was that this was a "crime of passion." That would take it from capital murder to second degree and save our boy from "riding the lightning," as the lawyer put it. The defendant readily admitted his guilt, was not insane, and was competent to stand trial. He'd blown his wife apart with a shotgun, after discovering she'd had at least three affairs in two months. One of her paramours was black, a total no-no in rural Alabama and just about the most offensive thing a wife could do to her husband. Further, this guy was literally a gangster who had shot up my guy's double-wide, rendering it unlivable. Then she'd laughed at him for getting her a pencil to sign the insurance check. That was what did it. He'd blasted her four times, with a thirty-aught-six, at point-blank range, right in front of her mother. He literally blew her into the next room. Psychological testing had confirmed that he was extremely depressed, angry, paranoid, and highly impulsive. It was an easy case. In fact, the defendant cried whenever he talked of his deceased wife. He'd forgiven her three times for her infidelity, and I really believe he was still hopelessly in love with her. Like I said, a crime of passion.

It was an easy case, until an ambitious young hot-shot from the State Attorney General's office decided to turn it into the Trial of the

Century. He didn't know I was coming to testify, not having bothered to check, so he insisted on his "voir dire" right to question me first without the jury. Then we did an encore with the jury back in the box. He examined me at length about the psychological tests, though they were standard instruments used routinely by all psychologists. He pranced up and down demonstrating his proficiency with the murder weapon, as he re-enacted the crime for my benefit and that of the jury. He insisted on showing me the gory photos of the victim's body, or what was left of it. He turned a twenty-minute pro forma testimony into a two-hour ordeal, all to rebut my testimony as to the obvious emotionality of this gruesome crime. The judge scolded him as I burned up the back roads back to Birmingham. I still missed my first afternoon appointment and remembered why I'd never developed much of a forensic practice. If there's ever a sequel to this book, it won't be *Tales from the Bench*. *Tales from the OR Table*, maybe.

What I'm trying to convey here is the incredible range of human beings, and of human experiences, that my work as a psychologist has exposed me to. I really never anticipated this when I chose my career, but I'm grateful for it. I've worked in community mental health centers, private practice offices, psychiatric hospitals, a VA alcohol program, a pain clinic, various courtrooms, and a family practice residency program, as well as day care centers, schools, college classrooms, and residential treatment facilities. I've held dozens of babies, wrestled with unruly adolescents, and sat in on open-heart surgery, close enough to reach out and grab a man's pulsating heart. I've lectured to high school and college kids, graduate students, family practice residents, my fellow psychotherapists, and public audiences. I've been interviewed a hundred times for newspapers and on radio and television programs. I've even made a few home visits. It turns out to have been a pretty broad "couch."

There have been a few unexpected twists along the way, even in my college teaching. I once took over a Personality course, six weeks into the semester, from another professor who was forced to retire for health reasons. I had taught it before and used the same text, so I was ready to go. But my colleague taught very differently. He simply read from the book instead of lecturing. He allowed special credit work, allowed skipping a test, and allowed some papers to be turned in early. The result was that some students had taken the first test, of which I had no copy, and some hadn't. Some knew their grades; some didn't. It took over a month to get the other man's test scores, papers, etc.—and when I tried to figure out what was what, the papers reeked so badly of nicotine that I had an allergic reaction. I had to air them out for several more weeks, so we were over half way through the semester before I got the mess sorted out. The class was, understandably, extremely worried about being treated fairly and knowing their grades. But we made it through the "Semester from Hell," for which I thanked the class, in relief, at the Final. Five minutes later, one of the students fell out of her chair, having a grand mal epileptic seizure. A nursing student took care of her, while another called 911. In ten minutes the room was full of firemen and medics, and the student was taken out on a gurney. The head of the emergency team asked if I was the professor. I admitted I was. "You give one helluva final exam, Doc," he said.

As a psychologist, I've had the rare privilege of working with people of all classes, races, creeds, professions, hobbies, perversions, phobias, and eccentricities imaginable. Pantie-freaks, doo-doo devils, and pigeon phobics, porno-addicts, philanderers and paranoids, all found their way to my door. I've seen people struggle to be successful against overwhelming odds, and win. Sometimes. I've seen people salvage marriages that were totally trashed and end up with peaceful, loving unions. Families have come in after losing children in horrible accidents, after loved ones have suicided, after alcohol and depression have ruined them. And they have survived. They have even learned, regrouped, and prospered. I see people at their very worst, but also at their best. I see the dregs of humanity but also how dignity, love, honor, pride, and compassion can prevail, even in the most troubled of our fellows.

As you've noticed, I've organized this book essentially around psychiatric diagnoses and treatments, with stories about patients with MPD, ADHD, personality disorders, etc. But all of it has been both case study and memoir. It's a story book. In this final chapter I hope you'll allow me to be a little more autobiographical and to focus more on other experiences of my psychology career.

Most notably, I need to tell you of the Hill Crest years. I had done my internship at PACE, working with adolescent males, and I loved it. But I wasn't so sure about inpatient work. This involves patients who are often very sick, in distress, and eager for help, a psychotherapist's cup of tea. But as a family therapist I had some qualms about inadvertently supporting a family's scape-goating of one member and supplying that person with a psychiatric diagnosis and a history of hospitalization. Think Hippocrates' "First, do no harm." On the other hand, these patients were going to be put in a hospital eventually, like it or not. So when Hill Crest Hospital sought to recruit me, I was willing to listen. There were other issues as well, such as being constantly on call and, of course, the increased liability of working with an inpatient population.

They set up an interview at my office and offered me the position of Clinical Director of the Adolescent Unit. There was also a Medical Director, Harry Mahannah, MD, but I was expected to develop and institute a new day-to-day treatment program. This was right up my alley, as I'd done very much the same thing on my internship. And the salary was exceptionally good. With some qualms, I accepted the half-time job. It led to some of the best years and most memorable experiences of my professional career. This could fill another whole book, and I've covered some of these anecdotes in earlier chapters, but please indulge me in just a few Hill Crest stories.

A sixteen-year-old wanted to escape and thought he could do so by breaking out a window. He slammed a picture window with a large terra cotta planter. Unfortunately for him, the window was not glass, but rather plexi-glass. It slammed the planter right back at him, without even cracking. We all gave him credit for a good try as we put him in restraints for the night.

Another kid came in with a cast on his arm, the result from hitting a wall at home. He got mad on the Unit and punched our wall with his other fist. Yup, both arms in full casts, a most inconvenient situation. "Sorry," said the nurses, "but we're psychiatric. We don't handle toilet problems." Turned out the wall was ¾-inch plywood, because Hill Crest was tired of repairing sheet rock. The patient didn't know that.

Once I came onto the Unit and one of the boys invited me to shoot a game of pool with him. I love the game and have a table at home. I'm competent but no pro, despite having met Minnesota Fats at a sales demonstration once. (Fats described breaking several tables learning to do a masse shot, then executed several perfectly.) The table was old, the felt threadbare, the cue tips barely visible, but I accepted as a courtesy to the patient, to develop rapport, that sort of thing. He graciously allowed me the break. I luckily sank the ten-ball on the break, then proceeded to run the table, finally calling and sinking the eight-ball. Poor kid never got a shot. I thanked him for a "good game," then sauntered off like I did this twice a day. I'd never run the table before and haven't since, but I'd instantly become a legend and wasn't about to let on.

I saw many fascinating patients there, many of whose stories are recounted in the preceding chapters. But in some ways the best part of my Hill Crest experience was working with the staff, the doctors, nurses, Occupational Therapists, other psychologists, counselors, and social workers. Dr. Les Alhadeff, the Hospital's Medical Director, became a good friend, along with his wife Debra. He was an over-grown kid himself, but very bright and capable. Artie Nelson was a talented Child Psychiatrist, rare in those days. Joe Frank Nuckols and I became good buddies. I remember strutting down the halls one day, whistling Mozart's "Eine Kleine Nacht Musik," when suddenly I heard somebody chime in with the counterpoint. It was Frank. The two of us marched gleefully down the corridor, whistling, to the awe and confusion of patients and staff alike.

One of my adolescent boys complained to me that his psychiatrist, Dr. Otto Eisenhart, would not talk with him. I was empathetic. Otto was tall, blond, handsome, and very Teutonic. He was abrupt, stern, and commanding by his very presence. He popped into the patient's room, acquired the medical information he required, and pounded out.

Intimidating to anybody, but especially a kid in a psychiatric hospital. But I knew something about Otto the patient didn't.

"Have you ever actually asked Dr. Eisenhart to talk with you?" I asked.

"No," he said. He was too afraid.

I suggested he try it. "You might be surprised, and you really have nothing to lose."

My next time on the Unit I looked him up and asked how things were going.

"I asked Dr Eisenhart to talk with me, " he replied.

"And?"

"He sat and talked with me for about forty minutes. He's a really cool guy."

I already knew that, but I was thrilled the kid had the guts to ask.

But best of all was my hooking up with Dr. James Barnett, who entered this narrative earlier in the book. A bearded black psychiatrist from Detroit, James has been talking for years about returning to the (former?) Motor City, but never did. Dr. Barnett had many adolescent patients, and so was required to attend my Unit team meetings. He is calm, low-keyed, respectful, knowledgeable, and genuinely caring. He's not much shocked by outrageousness and open to input from anybody. Perfect adolescent psychiatrist, and the patients loved him. He and I quickly formed a close friendship and excellent working relationship. We saw hundreds of patients at Hill Crest and Brookwood hospitals, both adolescent and adult.

It also turned out that he was a real hoot and that we brought out the best/worst in each other. We'd get together in team meeting, start cutting up, and soon have the whole team roaring with laughter. We were doing good clinical work, but at the same time we played off each other like a stand-up comedy team. Think Laurel and Hardy, Burns and Allen, etc. We literally had staff coming to meetings when they had no patients on the Unit, just to enjoy the show.

Ultimately Dr. Barnett became my closest professional associate. We referred to each other and worked together as a very close team.

He handled the medical side, me the psychotherapy (although he was always willing to talk with a patient and was good at it). He got me on staff at Brookwood Hospital, where he and I worked on the Eating Disorders Unit—possibly the toughest patients you can work with—along with unit Director Nancy Berland, Ph.D. Nancy and James are the undisputed local experts on anorexia and bulimia. It was a marvelous collaboration, and, if I may say so, we helped a lot of young girls, truly saving the lives of some. It also stimulated my practice enormously to see patients at two hospitals (three while I was teaching at Medical Center East, now St. Vincent's East) and follow up with them at the office. Those were the "Glory Years," and we knew we were fortunate.

Dr. Barnett came to my son's memorial service. "I knew you'd come, James," as I embraced him. I never doubted it. Since I was a small child no one has called me "Bobby," save a small handful who chose the nickname instinctively: Bobby DeBourbon, Dr. Steve Bair, and I suppose you could include my neighbor in Champaign, "Conkey," who inexplicably called me "Robbie."

I see him all too rarely, but when I do, James calls me Bobby.

As a psychologist I've often been called on to give public and private talks on various aspects of my work. Some I get paid; some are pro bono. The most lucrative was a professional presentation at a conference in San Francisco. They flew me from Birmingham to S.F. and back, all meals paid, plus a per diem, and $1,500 for an hour and a half speech. Plus free admission to the workshop, worth $500 and 20 education credits. My friend Dr. Paul Weir was also on the program, and I flew my wife out for a few days in one of our favorite cities.

One of the oddest and least expected talks was the unusual opportunity to address the Alabama Crimson Tide football team, the night before a big game. I don't remember who set it up (probably the Mental Health Association), but I dutifully showed up in Tuscaloosa to confront an audience of over a hundred players, coaches, etc. No doubt they were thinking of tomorrow's game and not the least interested in me, much less my appointed topic, suicide.

Why somebody wanted me to talk about suicide to a football team about to meet a tough opponent (I'm thinking Ole Miss or Mississippi St., but don't hold me to that) I'll never know. They must have thought it bizarre, and I certainly did. But I soldiered on and they listened pretty attentively, though I wondered if they thought I was suggesting *they* were suicidal for playing. Which I definitely did not.

After the talk, which I kept as brief and light as the topic would allow, several players came up and thanked me for coming, including their star running back, who I believe was called "Rocket." He was a very gracious and respectful young man. I believe he served some time in the NFL. I also met an assistant coach, who I asked about pro prospects for his players. "Well," he answered, "this *is* Alabama, so we'll send four or five a year." A sobering accounting, considering AL had one hundred players, few would survive their rookie year, and almost none for ten.

The Tide rolled over whoever it was the next night. I figured they'd have me back every week, but they never did. Probably wise; think how I might have subtly sabotaged their game plan psychologically. (Full disclosure: I'm an Auburn fan.) Unethical, of course, but we *are* talking college football here.

The practice of clinical psychology is a strange way to make a living. You spend a lot of time listening to people complain about how miserable they are when it is obvious that their lifestyles lead inevitably to anxiety, depression, and rage. Sometimes you just want to shake them and say, "Stop being so stupid and crazy." A lot of what you tell people is really just common sense. The art of psychotherapy comes in helping them get past whatever hang-up keeps them from acting in a reasonable and responsible fashion, as I learned from my family therapy friend Dr. Frank Pittman. We don't do surgery or even prescribe pills, and many therapists are understandably reluctant even to give much direct advice. Yet, we're expected to help people change behavior patterns and belief systems that have persisted for decades, deal with horrible tragedies, and save marriages that probably should never have happened in the first place. Oddly enough, we are often successful, by listening and truly understanding, by providing good sense perspectives in an accepting atmosphere, and by applying the findings of the science of human behavior. In fact, it is deeply ironic that "managed care" and other market-driven forces are systematically destroying psychology as a profession, just at the point where it has been able to provide solid scientific evidence that psychotherapy works.

Has thirty-six years of psychotherapy made me cynical, pessimistic, doubtful of the value of my species? Yeah, sometimes it has. Over all, though, I think I end up fairly well impressed with humanity. Not on a global, national, generic basis, where the worst of our simian, Tyrranosaurean nature gets expressed, but on the level of families, marriages, individuals. At that level, the level you see in the therapist's office, the goodness, "humanity," and adaptability of our species emerges. *People change.* I must believe that to do my job, but beyond belief I *see* it every day. In most of these tales, the protagonists came out on top. I'm glad I was there to see it.